MACCLESFIELD:
Those Were the Days

Doug Pickford

Published by Sigma Leisure - an imprint of
Sigma Press, 1 South Oak Lane, Wilmslow, Cheshire SK9 6AR, England.

British Library Cataloguing in Publication Data
A CIP record for this book is available from the British Library.

ISBN: 1-85058-423-0

Typesetting and Design by: Sigma Press, Wilmslow, Cheshire.

Cover design : The Agency, Wilmslow

The painting used on the cover is by Geoffrey Hunter and is based on a photograph of Mr & Mrs Harry Hancox provided by Jack Burgess. They are outside their Beech Lane premises in the 1950s and later went on to become licensees of the Leathers Smithy in Langley.

Printed by: Manchester Free Press

Preface

This book is dedicated, like *Macclesfield - So Well Remembered*, to Maxonians everywhere.

My thanks go to many people who have assisted and encouraged me in the compilation of these fond memories. My sincere thanks to all the kind folk who said how much they had enjoyed "Macclesfield, So Well Remembered" and the many who said I should (and must!) get another one together. This has been, for me, a labour of love and it has been delightful to meet so many old and new friends in the course of compiling this book. I am conscious that there is still much to be said about this wonderful town of Macclesfield and, perhaps, the future will hold further delights in this field, who knows? Everyone who has written for this book is, I trust, acknowledged and the vast majority of photographs are likewise acknowledged, I hope. If, however, I have failed to do so in any way then I beg your forgiveness. It is not a deliberate attempt to omit, but merely the failing of my memory.

Everyone who has assisted has provided their unique contribution to this publication and it would be wrong of me to single out anyone personally. Everyone has excelled. However, I am sure you will all agree that the painting on the front cover is quite delightful. I was looking through a number of photographs supplied by Mr Jack Burgess of Lyme Green one day and I showed one of them - of Mr and Mrs Harry Hancox - to a friend, Geoffrey Hunter. I mentioned to Geoffrey that I thought this would be ideal for the front cover. No sooner had I done so than he volunteered to paint a picture in water colours (a medium he had rarely used) from this. Over the weeks he would bring in his painting in various stages of completion for me to see and I became more and more delighted with his work as the days went by and really looked forward to seeing the next stage. The finished product can be seen on the front of this book and I am sure you will all agree that it is superb. I am happy to be able to say that the original now has pride of place in my lounge at home. I know that he spent many hours on this work, as others who have contributed have likewise done with theirs. For them all I know it has been a labour of love as it has been for me in getting these happy memories together. My thanks to each and every one.

Doug Pickford

Contents

1

Those Were the Days

There is no other township in the entire world like this Macclesfield of ours and there are no people in the entire world quite like Maxonians. They are, like this town, something rather special.

Outsiders have ripped the town apart, putting roads through it; demolishing hundreds upon hundreds of homes and even pulling down an Infirmary for a supermarket. It is my view that a lot of what has taken place was an unnecessary attempt to destroy the old Treacle Town. But the attempt has been unsuccessful – thanks to the people of this fair town. On the surface they have demolished this and pulled down that and they have ruined this and changed that ... but it is *under* the surface that matters. It is there that there can be found people's memories and people's hearts; it is the Macclesfield spirit that prevails, no matter what.

The good times were there and the good times can still be here thanks to our memories.

In 1993 I had the idea of collecting memories of Macclesfield people and putting them together in a book that I called, *Macclesfield, So Well Remembered* alluding to the film made by Hollywood and set in Macclesfield just after the second world war called *So Well Remembered.* People still recall the film stars coming to town and a lot of locals were used as extras. The book proved to be very popular, I am pleased to say, and no sooner had it hit the bookshelves than I was being asked to compile another one. And here it is.

I described it as "pure, unashamed nostalgia" and offered no apologies whatsoever for wallowing in those happy times when the sun always shone, front and back doors could be left open and everyone knew everyone. True, there was little money about for most people but that mattered not one jot. Everyone was in the same boat and so there was no competition like there is today. There was no "keeping up with the Joneses" apart from everyone keeping their front steps as clean as the next person's. But that was a matter of pride. Everyone knew their place and there was a place for everyone. Holidays were taken at Barnaby and holiday savings were drawn out just before Barnaby at the Co-op. The divi was part of life and we couldn't do without it. And when we went to Blackpool or wherever for a few days or a week we all knew everyone when we got off the train ... for it was the time of year when Macclesfield moved to the seaside. Very few stayed behind; those who did were cleaning the boilers at the mills or were part of a family too large to travel at one time. There were many large families then. The pill was something for the future.

Washing day was Monday. All the families hung out their clothes on the line after a good rinse in the dolly tub with Dolly Blue applied to the whites. When it was sunny the aspidistra plants were carried out from the front room windows and were given an airing; Friday was fish and chips day and Sundays seemed to be for Granelli's ice cream.

The pictures changed twice a week (except sometimes the Majestic which showed the main pictures for an entire week shortly after release). We had to wait a few months before they came round again and were shown at the Premier (pronounced Preemier) or the 'Drome or the Cinema or the Regal. The Majestic was posh and cost more than the others. Saturday was the kids' matinee when the cliff-hanger serials always left the hero to a dangerous fate worse than death but, amazingly, the following week he (or she) always got away. Without fail.

Then there were the war years; strong and powerful memories prevail for this period in history; for some they were sad. Menfolk did not return. We still weep for them. But others – especially the youngsters around when war broke out – recall the time with nostalgia. The Yanks billeted around the town brought chewing gum and bee-bop. The didn't like our warm beer and were not allowed to drink our milk. Both were their loss, not ours.

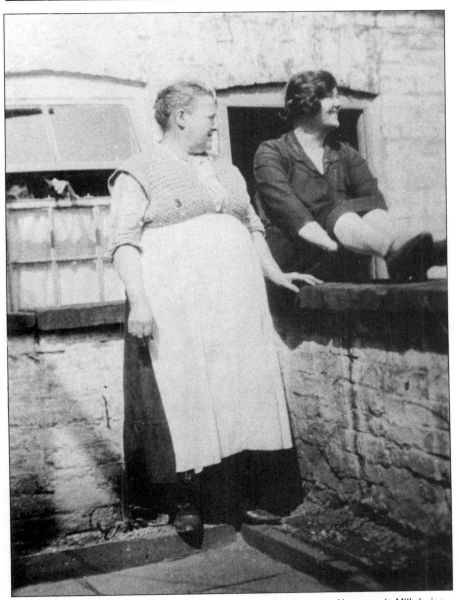

Mary "Polly" Burgess in her back yard at 14 London Road, next to Hewetson's Mill during the 1920s. Her daughter, Amy, is sitting on the wall. (J. Burgess)

And today, there are some Macclesfield ladies in distant parts of the United States, war brides who sailed to the other side of the Atlantic to be reunited with their loves. A number of copies of the last book went over to America to these Maxonians – proof again that memories of Macclesfield never die. They do not even fade away ... they grow stronger with the passing years.

This time I have included contributions from Maxonians exiled in Australia and in lovely Cornwall, not to mention Bradford and Biddulph! It is their memories that keep the old town very much alive. They may have moved but they have not forgotten.

So there we are. May I please extend a warm and cordial invitation for you to, once again, come with me on a journey. A journey back in time. A journey to Old Macclesfield where once again those happy days are re-lived in words and in pictures. Many of the photographs used in this book have never been published before. They are the treasured possessions of people who wish to share them with you. They are beautiful and they are delightful.

Once again, this book is dedicated to the warm-hearted folk of Macclesfield whether they are living far or near. They are the salt of the earth and the pride of Cheshire.

Yes, those were the days ... please re-live them once more as we look at Macclesfield, so well remembered.

Opposite: Amy Burgess (pictured on the previous photograph on the back yard wall) in London Road approaching Byrons Lane, looking towards the town, with tiny niece Beryl. They are outside the first house past the Sunday School. In the background can be seen the Salt Man, most probably "Yok Salt" who was a familiar figure around Macclesfield. He would saw off required lumps of salt from the big block he carted around.

2

Once Upon a Time in Macclesfield

Sound of horse's clip-clop, clip-clop hooves,
Wheels that rolled in well-worn grooves;
Mill walls muting looms' loud clatter,
Housewives at the door in friendly chatter.

Not like endless modern traffic roar,
Sounds in streets were homelier, lower.
No fear for children playing there, except
A bolting horse down on them swept.

Young Tom in bed with sneezing cold
Listens to the street cries, O, so old,
"Line props", "Salt", and "Grimsby fish",
"Fresh watercress", bring out your dish.

Hello! Rare excitements in the street,
Organ man, his monkey's nimble feet;
Bear that dances chained to pole,
And one-man band; yes, upon my soul.

Printed bills proclaim circus is in town,
Beating drum, blaring band, funny clown,
Man on stilts, dwarf in need of stilts,
Horses, tigers, lions – imagination wilts.

A penny for the singer in the street,
Her old clothes, peeping toes, tired feet.
Dismal notes from cornet now arose,
Much beer flowed to colour his nose.

O, come to the fair on Waters Green,
To its garish lights and crowded scene.
Painted horses whirl in endless chain,
First films flicker like silver rain.

Town bellman rings his bell so loud
Soon he is ringed – by a curious crowd.
What's his news? Little child is lost,
Or ring, less precious what 'ere it cost.

Dusk, then darkness, decree day's close,
Lamplighter's torch, street lamp glows;
All asleep, save watchman in his hut,
Policeman a-foot sees doors are shut.

Peaceful is the street on Sabbath Day,
Good folk in church, no children play,
Distant music of Salvation Army Band,
Old, sweet story of the Promised Land.

Philip Murray

3

Billy Cans and Roman Baths

I often go walking in the hills above Macclesfield with Maurice Winnell, who was born in Barton Street. During our travels he will sometimes tell me a story or two about his early days in the twenties and thirties in Old Macclesfield.

It was on a glorious sunny day as we walked past Wincle Grange that Maurice spoke of the 'Roman Baths' and I asked him or his memories to be shared. These they are:

"As a lad in the 1920s and 1930s the nearest we came to computer games was a game of Ludo or Snakes and Ladders bought as a Christmas present (along with a 2/6p Cadbury's selection box). So our entertainment was self produced and usually outdoors if weather permitted. In the early 1930s on sunny Saturdays during the summer our little gang of lads made our way across The Turf Moss, along the canal to Fool's Nook and Hawkshead quarry. Deserted by the workmen at weekends it was a wonderland to explore, accompanied by a stray dog picked up along the way.

"We spent many happy carefree hours and used a First World War billy can to fry eggs and bacon over a little wood fire (a mixture of mashed up egg, bacon and smuts) nothing ever tasted better washed down with a penny bottle of lemonade. Sometimes we would say, "Let's go to look at the Roman Baths". This was upstream from the quarry, a stone weir made to divert water from the stream along a culvert to feed Bosley Reservoir, built in the early 1800s. We knew nothing of its true age or reason for construction and were firmly convinced that it was a Roman Baths, a conviction held by all other lads who knew of it.

"While walking to and fro along the canal we made boats out of reeds by bending the point over and sticking it through the flat part, with the wind blowing them along we had races.

"As lads roaming the countryside another expedition was to White Nancy overlooking Bollington. I remember as a lad of about 10 climbing to White Nancy, it then had an open doorway and inside a stone table in the middle and a stone seat around the wall, a very small place as you can imagine. One of my friends had a relation who worked at White Nancy Laundry in Bollington so in my young mind I thought it was the one and the same place (I could not see how they could manage to do the laundry in such a tiny building).

"We used to visit the windmill on the side of Kerridge, a tapering stone tower with no sails and it was demolished during the Second World War.

"As lads we walked everywhere and we thought nothing of walking from Macclesfield through Sutton, past Cleulow Cross to Dane Valley, that was usually our Easter walk. We made our way down along the river and part way along the feeder towards Rushton. We took sandwiches and lemonade and I remember we played on a punt on the feeder which was normally used by the Keeper to maintain the banks etc. Many Macclesfield people spent a day at Easter in Dane Valley picnicking. They caught the bus to Cleulow Cross or Wincle Church but as lads we had no threepennies for fares so we walked there and back.

"We occasionally visited a mound in the middle of the Turf Moss which in bygone years had been used by the old volunteers as a place for target practice. We dug the spent bullets out of it. This place for target practice was used before the Rulow Hollow range came into being to be used in the First World War. We knew the firing steps on the hillside there and from the back ones it looked a very long distance to the target hillside.

"We spent a lot of time in the South Park and we would look for a plant with feathery white flowers that had small nuts at the root; we called them pig nuts and we dug them up, washed them off in the park drinking fountain and ate them. They resembled small hazelnuts. We also chewed small oval leaves off a smaller plant and called them vinegar leaves, they did have a distinct vinegar taste.

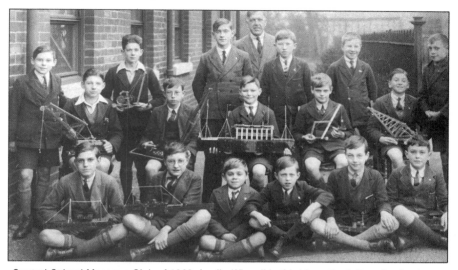

Central School Meccano Club of 1932. Leslie Winnell is third from the left on the front row. The teacher is Mrs Coups, woodwork and music master. (M Winnell)

"We reckoned we could tell the time of day by the number of puffs it took to blow all the seeds off a dandelion head and a buttercup held under a friend's chin determined if they liked butter or not by the amount of reflected yellow shown under their chin.

"To smoke out a wasps' nest, we wrapped old celluloid film in brown paper, set it alight, stamped the flames out and then stuffed the very smoking remains up into the wasps' nest with a turf to block the entrance. After a short interval we would dig the wasp cake out and use the wasp maggots for fishing. Needless to say, our method was not 100 per cent effective and we suffered the odd sting or two.

"South Park was our normal play area but we occasionally visited the other parks in town, we played on the two big cannons in the West Park, swarming along the barrel. The cannons were brought back from Sebastopol after the Crimean War, unfortunately they were melted down for scrap during

World War Two along with the town's ancient iron stocks which I remember within some railings also in the West Park.

"We collected seed heads from a plant and called them sticky bobs, in spite of the name we gave them they were not sticky but consisted of a mass of tiny hooks to cling onto any rough passing surface. We stood at the bottom of Barton Street and many unsuspecting people went on their way along Brown Street with one or two attached to their back.

"In the days before mechanisation, the street grids were cleaned out by a man equipped with a hook to lift the grid, and a metal scoop fixed onto a long wooden handle to lift the silt out for removal. If we lost anything down a grid we would watch out for the grid cleaner to arrive to try and recover our lost article.

"As a young lad, I was the proud possessor of a pair of black hard leather gaiters. They fitted from ankle to just below the knee and fastened on the outside with a pair of straps and buckles, a full size version was sometimes worn by farmers and milkmen etc. All the family at our house had a pair of galoshes to slip over their shoes to cope with the slush of melting snow; they were very popular in the 1920s – 1930s.

"With our Saturday penny we bought and chewed liquorice root (like a shrivelled brown twig), tiger nuts and small black pods named Lotus pods.

"The Walls' ice cream man peddled round on his three wheeled bike with the large square ice cream container between the front two wheels, on it was a slogan 'Stop Me and Buy One'. Granelli's ice cream was sold from a two wheeled barrow pushed around the streets and a hand bell rung to announce its arrival.

"During the appropriate season we had conker competitions; we had several ways to harden our favourite conker such as soaking in vinegar, roasting in the oven etc and if we were lucky we could boast a conker over 50 or 60 by shattering all opponents' conkers. Dare I admit it, after all these years, that sometimes we had a steel nut tied on the other end of the string and with sleight of hand it would shatter all other conkers and never be noticed. (There -- our secret is out!)"

11

A familiar shop in Macclesfield before the war ... Wardle's Mantle Manufacturers, opposite Woolworths in Mill Street.

"Bonfire night was much looked forward to and for a few nights before the event we went round the neighbours collecting money to buy fireworks. As an effort to impress likely donators we used a shoe box with a design pricked out through the lid, a lit candle was fixed inside and with the box held lid-forwards quite an impressive picture would be illuminated through the perforations. My favourite was an impression of Mow Cop probably because we had a picture on the wall at home of that scene. We used to chant a rhyme which went something like this:

> *Bonfire night is coming, the pigs are getting fat;*
> *Please spare a penny for the old man's hat.*
> *If you haven't got a penny a ha'penny will do*
> *If you haven't got a ha'penny then God bless you.*

"Looking back to boyhood days it comes to mind how much enjoyment we had from simple pursuits, although we had little money and few possessions our lives were rich in the pleasures of our adventures and the friendships we formed with similar aged lads, which continued into adult life.

4

When the World was a Much Happier Place

Percy Wardle of Countess Close came to Macclesfield in 1926 with his parents and lived on the newly-built Buxton Road estate. When he put pen to paper about the Macclesfield he so well remembers he wrote, "This happened in times when the world was a much happier place to live in".

Later, when I had a chat with him, he reminisced that in Macclesfield in those days it was normal to have doors either open or unlocked. There was little or no crime. He told me: "I remember someone leaving their wages in a mill. When they came back to work after the weekend the envelope with their money in was still there."

You could not do that now, I fear, but there was the occasional 'shady' character as well as Percy recalls:

"For six months in 1927, I worked part-time for a Mr Fox who had a furniture shop in Old Park Lane and a two-storey workshop in the yard behind the shop, where he made the furniture. My job was two hours after school, sanding the various pieces, with no mechanical sanders to help. It was hard manual work.

"Cash sales were few and far between, and H.P. relatively unknown, the order of the day was a few bob down (and without signed agreements) and pay a little each week. Therefore it was essential that the customers correct address was checked, especially when the customer was taking something with him, like a chair or gramophone. So on odd occasions Mr Fox would come into the workshop and say, "Leave the sanding and follow

13

the customer I have in the shop". Then, feeling like Sherlock Holmes, I would slip across the road to the newsagent's window, which was directly opposite, and wait for the customer to leave. On one occasion I followed a customer from the shop to Fountain Street where he went down an entry where I assumed he lived. I did not know Macc too well in those days, as I did not arrive here to live until 1926.

"Feeling quite happy I went back and reported to Mr Fox, who then told me the man had given a Moss Rose address, and to make matters worse the entry in Fountain Street went straight through to Buxton Road. To this day, I do not know if he was ever found!"

Later, he went to work for Maypole Grocers in Mill Street. It was 1928 and he writes:

"I was still attending school, the job was Saturdays only and consisted of delivering groceries through Bollington Cross, then through Bollington itself, and back along Clarke Lane and on to Macc. I had a key to the shop yard, and every Saturday morning at 8.30 a.m. I would unlock the yard gate and there waiting was a box type hand cart which was loaded to the brim with parcels of groceries, all labelled for delivery. I would set off (wet or fine) and trundle the cart to Bollington, making deliveries on the way. At noon I used to stop at a cafe at the top of Water Street, and buy a cup of tea and eat my own sandwiches." (Fancy trying that nowadays.)

"By the time I arrived at Lord Street, three-quarters of the parcels had been delivered, and a good job too, for the hill was far too steep for a loaded cart. Even today, whenever I see Lord Street, I still wonder how on earth I ever pulled that cart to the top. I would pull the cart up the hill for about 15 yards, then let the wheels run back to the kerb which I had a breather. This way, plus about three stops for deliveries, finally got me to the top. One day I was half way up the hill and having one of my various rests, when a lady who was passing by stopped, and told me she was going to complain to the Maypole as she considered the job was far too heavy for me. She did complain too, for when I finally arrived back at the shop, and drew my pay, which was 3/6d for the day, the manager gave me verbal notice, and with a fond farewell I was gone!"

5

Sunday Papers at the Central Station

Seventy-eight years old Mr D Scott used to live in Smyth Street, Macclesfield, during the 1920s but later moved to Biddulph Moor. These are some of his memories:

"I remember when we had no bus station and no ambulances like we have today. Now I wonder if I might enlighten you as regards the job of newsboys in the 1920s. I was employed as a newsboy by Mr J.B. Chapman of 78 Chestergate seven days a week.

"My day started at 5.15 a.m. when my father woke me, when I got up and had a wash. I then went downstairs to a warm fire and a cup of warm tea. It was then time to go to Hibel Road Station with my box on wheels to meet the Paper Train.

"I would then go to the various agents for the papers which were put into the box on wheels, then when this was full I would push this box up the slope from the station and on to Hibel Road, Jordangate, Market Place, then down Chestergate to the shop. Here the papers were taken out and put on to the counter. I would then gather the papers I needed for my round.

"My round started at the bottom of Prestbury Road then into Risely Street, Prestbury Road as far as the West Park Hospital known in those days as the Work House, then back down Prestbury Road and on to Chester Road, Oxford Road, Cottage Street, Crompton Road, Athey Street, West Bond Street, Catherine Street, then back to the shop.

"It was then home for my breakfast and then catch the school bus from Gladstone Square. In the evening I would go

15

down again to the station for the Evening Chronicle, we did this every day until Friday. Saturday was a little different. The early morning paper as usual then about 10 a.m. down to the station to pick up a single sheet newspaper which had all the racing in and was known ad the Mid-day Chron. (or One O'clock to those who back horses).

"In the evening down to the station again for the Evening Chronicle, an hour later down to the station again, this time for the 'Evening Chronicle Football Final'. After all this I would then have to go to the Central Station and pick up the 'Evening Sentinel Football Final'. This paper came by road.

"On Sunday the Sunday Papers came to the Central Station from Manchester. I would go once again to the various agents for the papers we required which were loaded into the box on wheels, then once again up to the shop, but this time not up Hibel Road, but through Waters Green and UP, yes UP Church Wallgate, then on to the shop. My sister came on Sunday and helped to push this box of papers up the hill. Can you imagine the newsboys of today doing this?"

He asked me: "Have you ever looked out of your office across Chestergate and seen something unusual and rare? No? Well just look at John Douglas' window. I am firmly convinced that this window is the one of the two bow windows that belonged to John Green Provision Shop. John Green's shop was the only double-bowed window in Chestergate and was situated just where John Douglas is."

6

Working at The Top Shop and memories of Madam Ellis

Believe it or not, Eric Sherratt and I first met one Saturday afternoon at Buxton Market. We had both been 'taken shopping' by our respective spouses and had ended up in the Peak District for a change. Eric saw me and, I'm pleased to say, introduced himself as being from Macclesfield. A firm friendship has developed since, and he has loaned me a number of treasured family photographs.

One he brought to me I found particularly interesting. It showed his aunt, Laura Wyatt, and her daughter Maggie outside their house at 13 Davies Street, a house now, of course, demolished, like so many others (unnecessarily in my view).

Eric also wrote the following:

"Laura was born on the 12th April 1881 at Court 1, Lord Street, Sutton, Macclesfield. She was born to Eliza Thompson and her father was Frank Thompson. He worked as an operative silk dyer.

"In 1891 when Laura was 10 years old she started work at what was known as the 'Top Shop', Brocklehurst Whiston Amalgamated Ltd. The 'Top Shop' was on Fence Avenue. Laura worked from early morning until lunch time, then in the afternoon she attended school. Her job at the factory during the whole of her working life was that of winder.

"At the age of 23 on the 24th of December 1904, she was married at St Paul's Church to Arthur Wyatt who was a farm labourer and later went to work for Welch's coal merchant.

17

Arthur delivered coal to his customers from a flat cart drawn by a Shire horse. The horse was stabled in Welch Street, I often went to the stables with him, that was a treat I looked forward to.

Laura Wyatt and her daughter Margaret (Maggie) outside their house, 13 Davies Street. (Eric Sherratt)

"Getting back to Laura, who continued to work for Brocklehurst Whiston until she retired at turned 70: she was presented with a clock from her workmates and a cheque from B.W.A. for her long service. The presentation was made by Mr R.H.S. Aspinall, General Manager.

"During the whole of her working life she went to work wrapped in a shawl. It is interesting to note that Uncle Arthur always knew what to buy Laura for Christmas – it was invariable a new shawl. I will always remember her in her shawl.

"When I was about 12 years old, Laura would send me to the back door of the Bull Inn which was on the Dumbar (the front door being on Buxton Road). She would give me a jug with a cloth over it for it to be filled with a gill of beer. I never knew if it was for Uncle Arthur or Auntie Laura.

"Margaret started work when she was 14 years old. She also worked for Brocklehurst Whiston starting at the 'Middle Shop' which was in Bowden Street. She worked for B.W.A. for 40 years until she retired. Laura and Margaret between them completed over 100 years service for Brocklehurst Whistons.

"I will close now with a few words about number 13 Davies Street. Davies Street was situated between Waterloo Street and Buxton Road. On the photograph can be seen the grid on the pavement, through which Uncle Arthur would drop the coal into the cellars. In the window can be seen an Aspidistra, a plant popular in those days.

"In the cellar was an archway and supposedly a tunnel, it is said that this was an 'escape route' leading to the Castle where Mothercare now stands. The tunnel had been bricked up for many years ... "

Talking of Castles ... here is a list of premises in Castle Street, Macclesfield, I recall from 1955: 2/4 – J Mottershead Fruiterer; 6 – Marrion's Ladies Hairdressers; 8 – H.H. Holland Fish & Game Dealer, Back entrance to Black's Head Hotel; 10 – Halifax Building Society, Parking ground for Elwood Silk Ltd; 12 – Pimlott Jeweller; 14 – Macclesfield Times & Courier Ltd, Newspaper Proprietor; 14 – Lockwood, Gents' Tailor & Outfitter; Castle Street – Chambers, G.C. Kirk Solicitor; 18 – Shepley House Rainwear; 20 – Stanley Hall Chambers, Women's Union

Assurance, Provincial Insurance, London & Manchester Assurance; 24 – May Etchell's Cafe; 26 – Miss M.A. Morley, Ladies' Outfitters; 28 – Stanley Hall; Macclesfield Conservative Association for Dances and Entertainment; 30 – Nouvelle Dancing Studio; 32 – P Wellings, Chemist; 34 – General Post Office (Head Office).

Eric Sherratt outside the family shop in Buxton Road.

Who, I wonder, remembers Macclesfield's famous fortune-teller and palmist 'Madam Ellis'? Eric certainly does, for she was a friend of his mother's in the 1930s and 1940s. Eric remembers:

"Madam Ellis, palmist, kept a haberdashery shop at 45 Buxton Road. She came to Macclesfield from Blackpool in the late 1930s. In Blackpool she had her palmist business on the promenade.

Another shot of Sherratt's grocers, Buxton Road, about 1950.

"When the May and Wakes fairs came to Macclesfield she occupied a tent in Water's Green at the bottom of the slope leading to Central Station. Here she would tell the fortunes of her clients and would continue to do this from her shop in Buxton Road throughout the rest of the year.

"Her tent, although small, consisted of two 'rooms'. An outer reception area had two chairs and the inner consulting room had two further chairs, a small round table and all the necessary equipment for her business.

"The outer part of the tent was very brightly decorated with Madam Ellis' name over the door, on each side of which was a glass case containing photographs of celebrities who had sought her counsel. During quiet periods she would sit outside her tent, and what a colourful character she made dressed in traditional Gypsy costume.

21

"Madam Ellis was married to a Mr Freeman until one night a tragedy occurred. A gas leak in the shop resulted in Mr Freeman losing his life. His wife, although very ill at the time, survived, and in due course married a Mr Gibson."

An advert for Madam Ellis, Palmist, September 14th, 1939. The other adverts shown are very interesting ... war was imminent and there was an offer of war risk insurance by J. Stonier, Insurance Specialist, Brunswick Street.

Opposite: *Fred and Nellie Mellor owned the shoe shop in Buxton Road next door to Madam Ellis's shop. Pictured is the then Margaret Mellor aged about nine in the 1940s with her friend Marie Jones. Madam Ellis, Margaret recalled, sold various items including Beechams Powders, baby powder, razor blades, peas, matches and cigarettes. Margaret's father wouldn't allow her to wear ankle socks until the 1st of June every year so she used to cut them to ankle length! The day on which this photograph was taken was a Wednesday afternoon because the shop is shut for half day closing. The blinds are down. Madam Ellis was well remembered by Margaret. She used to have a tent whenever the fair visited Macclesfield and people would come to the shop to have their palms read or the future told in the cards.*

7

China Dog wi' Six-Week-Owld Pups on the Chimbley Piece

I could not let this volume go without a piece of 'Macc Chat' by my, alas, departed mentor and colleague, the late Philip Murray. Philip delighted countless thousands with his writing in Macclesfield dialect and, thanks to the kind offices of his nephew, Mr John Snape, I am pleased to be able to reproduce one of them here. The narrative is between two elderly Maxonians and is an absolute delight!

"It isna only that Maxfilt's changed on th' outside," said pensioner Bill. "If tha goes inside th' 'ouses they're nowt like what we knowed in th' owld days.

Joe: Lookin' from where Ahm sittin', tha's still got some things tha should 'ave throwed out donkey's 'ears ago.

Bill: Includin' thee.

Joe: Ah didna 'ear that. But when Ah looks back an' pictures th' 'omes me an' thee lived in as lads, Ah thinks a lot o' folk today, specially th' younger end, doesna know they're well off.

Bill: Nowt but tiles on livin' room floor in our 'ouse, 'cept for th' 'earthrug. Kitchen were flagged. Womenfolk pegged th' rug. Fireplace tha blackleaded, fender tha shined wi metal polish an' wasna allowed to rest thi feet on it.

Joe: On one side o' fireplace blow-bellers was 'ung on a nail; toastin' fork on tother side. Remindin' thee o' toast for tay on a winter day wi good beef drippin' an' a pinch o' sault on th' toast.

24

Bill: When tha biled th' iron kettle for a cup o' tay, smoke sometimes got down spout, resultin' in smoked tay. Tasted like tha'd sugared it wi a tayspoonful o' soot.

Joe: Granny's 'ouse was lit by a ile lamp on th' table. If tha wanted a read, tha drawed up to th' table. Went to bed by candle-light.

Bill: Ah remembers early days o' gaslight. Work o' art puttin' on th' mantle. If tha touched it, tha busted it. Scientific way was thredin' a knittin' needle through th' top an' lowerin' it gently.

Joe: Then tha could see th' pictures on wall, includin' if tha wasna a 'eathen a text from th' Good Book an' a calendar.

Ornaments on th' chimbley piece wasn'a complete wi'out a china dog wi six-week-old pups which never growed up.

Bill: 'Earthrug was shifted on bath night in case watter was spilled. If tha'd built up th' fire, tiles were warm an' didna chill thi feet when tha stepped out. After emptyin', tin bath was 'ung on a nail in th' backyard.

Joe: Biler fire in kitchen was kindled on weshin' day. Watter ladled into wash-tub wi ladlin' can. Clothes given a good 'idin' wi dolly peg. Manglin' follered.

Bill: Weshin' day one o' mi earliest memories. Shooed me off when Ah toddled near th' wash-tub, which drawed me like a magnet. Stone floor soppin' wet, clouds o' steam, swish an' thump o' dolly peg, mangle janglin', an' smell o' soapsuds an' wet clothes. Lentil soup and tater pie on dinner menu.

Joe: Firegrates in th' bedrooms. If someone were in bed wi a cowld, a shovelful o' burnin' coal from livin' room fire was carried upstairs to warm th' room.

Bill: They rubbed thee front an' back wi camphorated ile so cowld wouldna settle on thi chest. Poultice in severe cases. Piece o' flannel lapped round thi neck for sore throat. Cure completed wi lemon tay an' spoonfuls o' glycerine.

Joe: Sunday tay was special. Custard in best glass; bowl o' stewed prunes, rhubub, apples, or pineapple chunks. Cheshire cheese.

Bill: Windin' up wi a slice o' bunloaf, which were currant bread second class, currants bein' few an' far between. Improvement on seed cake dry as sawdust. When tha 'ad seed cake tha prayed th' tay for weshin' it down wasna smoked.

Joe: When they packed thee off to bed on a winter night it were perishin' cowld in th' bedroom. But childer soon got warm by sleepin' back to back.

Bill: One o' th' compensashuns in a big family. It were a struggle for parents, but Ah thinks it were worth all th' care an' strivin'. All them childer, wi their different looks an' little ways, growin' up around thee an', in course o' time, gettin' grandchilder as second editions o' th' first printin'.

Ah recollects a little lad lookin' up to 'is mother an' sayin': "When Ahm a man, Ah'll buy thee a beautiful silk dress." Was they listenin' in th' silk mills?

Buxton Road in the very early 1960s just above where the preceding photos were taken. Watling's Motor Cycle Shop was a familiar sight.

8

Poacher's Broth at the Fur & Feathers

Here's a question I know some readers may be able to answer: Why was the public house on Moss Lane referred to as the Fur and Feathers during the 1930s? The answer is that it was the meeting place for most of the poachers in Macclesfield!

Another haunt of the Macclesfield poachers was the Navigation at the top of Saville Street in those days now so long gone, but so well remembered.

Several years ago I had the pleasure of listening to some tales of poaching for rabbits in the Macclesfield of yesteryear from a gentleman still very much alive and kicking but I'd better not give his name or address just in case there's anyone still about with old scores to settle against these lads who went out by moonlight to net the rabbits in the fields around Macclesfield. What I will say about him is that he was born and bred in Saville Street around the year 1925. In that street at that time in just 13 houses there were 72 children living in conditions that must have been appalling. The two-up and two-downs were not exactly spacious. Times were hard and that is why, I am told, poaching was a favourite pastime for a number of young lads and their fathers as well. Not only did it fill plenty of bellies but the meat could also be sold. My "Mr X" used to go around Macclesfield with a barrow full of rabbits for sale. All the policemen were known by name because they arrested the poachers so often. The usual punishment was a fine of 14 days in Strangeways. As there was little money it was usually the 14 days in Strangeways Hotel. "You never said your dad had gone away for 14 days" he told me, "you always said a fortnight!

The poachers carried home-made nets and a stick hidden under their coats. The stick was for killing the animal and the nets for catching them. He remembers such characters as Nigger Naden and Cockney Harry and most of the Saville Street Gang were rehoused around the Moss. When my friend went there in the thirties the rent was 6/9d a week.

"There wasn't much work about then" he said. "That's why we all had to have a go at poaching. But our dads always found money for their beer. They got their priorities right!

Someone who well remembered Macclesfield's famous, or infamous, poachers was the late Philip Murray of Buxton Road, for many years a distinguished Macclesfield journalist. Back in 1987 Philip told me some of his memories of those "Rappit" poachers. He had read an article of mine and his thoughts had been taken to the Saville Street area where his father once pointed out nets hanging from a clothes line in a yard and said to young Philip: "What do you think they are?" and Philip answered: "Fishing nets", to which his father said: "No, they are rabbit poachers' nets. The men must have been out last night and they are drying their nets.

Soon the young Mr Murray was to meet a gang of poachers. Fishing the canal at Gurnet one evening he heard the distant tramp of feet. Looking along the towpath, he saw a gang of men rapidly approaching.

As they passed he saw their jackets bulging with nets hidden underneath. On they marched in the direction of London Road. They, too, were going fishing ... for rabbits.

An elegant variation in the pronunciation of the word "rabbit" was favoured by some men not of Macclesfield's intellectual elite. "Rappits", they said.

Rabbits were plentiful. Philip told me that returning one evening with his father after fishing Redesmere they came to a field in which were dozens of them. Putting two fingers into his mouth, his father produced an ear-splitting whistle. There was a wild flurry of white tails and in a instant not a rabbit could be seen.

As a trainee reporter with the *Macclesfield Times* Philip was too young to go into police court. But not too young to be sent to a solicitor's office to copy the summonses in cases for hearing in the County Police Court in King Edward Street. One summons was for poaching and in it was the phrase "coming from land there in pursuit of game, to wit (namely) conies.

What the devil conies were, he had no idea. Later he learned that "conies" was apparently a legal term for rabbits, a definition confirmed in a dictionary.

He reported many cases of poaching heard in the Borough and County Police Courts, and his impression was that poachers preferred the Borough Bench to the county where the landed interest was strong and presumably more sensitive to trespass.

One night, a group of anglers was returning from Langley reservoirs. Passing Langley wood, where the road was very dark, they were accosted by a man with a rabbit for sale. Philip's father bought it. When he reached home he discovered the rabbit was a black one.

"Oh," mother exclaimed, "we can't eat that. It will be like eating our black cat.

Marine store dealers in Macclesfield paid a penny for each rabbit sold to them.

Next two pages: *One of the highlights of the year during the 1930s was the choosing and crowning of Macclesfield Silk Queens, also known as the Silk Queen of Great Britain. Two of the town's royal ladies ... Lillian Jarvis pictured left, processing in South Park in 1931 and , right, Brenda Goodwin.*

9

West-Ward Ho!

Mike and Chris Dorey now live in Penzance, although both have their roots firmly set here in Macclesfield (and Bollington). Mike is of the well-known family of Doreys who many will remember for their fruit and veg shop in Park Lane – or to give it its Maxonian name, OLD Park Lane. His father, Walter, was a well-known musician as well. His wife, Chris, is a Bollingtonian with many happy memories of Macclesfield.

Early in 1994 they both got in touch and sent me their contributions to these memories. Chris also sent a copy of a delightful painting of Brunswick Hill. This is Mike Dorey's journey back into his early Macclesfield days which he has entitled "West-Ward Ho!

"The centre of every child's universe is – or should be – home. For me, home was 32 Chester Road, from where life drew me inexorably into its web during the 1930s, '40s and '50s.

"Under the watchful eyes of my parents and maternal grandparents, the seeds of discipline and good manners were sown. There was no confusion about right and wrong. Right was what you were told to do, wrong was what you were told not to do. The system was almost foolproof because everyone involved in implementing it had the same yardsticks. A clip round the ear or a well placed boot, a very strong warning or the ultimate visit to one's parents, all acted as deterrents. Whether it was the 'Parkie', a neighbour or policeman, the same rules applied and it was sensible to take notice of those ominous words "I know your father, laddie.

"There was also the chief constable, Mr Sheasby. he would walk along Chester Road, as he went to and from his office. He was ramrod straight and had eyes like gimlets. If you saw him, even if you weren't doing anything wrong, you checked to make sure, just in case.

"In those days, even the youngest children could 'play-out' in the street, without fear of deviants and only occasionally having to dodge the milkman or coalman with their horses and carts.

"Although we played 'French cricket', in Hall Street, Longacre Street and Hope Street West and proper cricket and footie in St Alban's schoolyard, our real territories became what were called 'Down't Lane', 'On't tip', The Workhouse Fields, West Park and the cemetery.

"'Down't Lane' was the bottom of Hope Street West, past the coal yard, where the air-raid shelters were. 'On't tip' was just above and led to the old skating rink, where Mr and Mrs Bason held sway and where we were allowed to feed the hens and play, until the war came and it was used for storing aircraft – under guard I might add – although it didn't always stop us sneaking on for a look. Eventually we strayed further afield but first we had to handle school.

"Christ Church was hardly a stone's throw from 'our 'ouse' and I remember we had a game. We stood on the footpath and taking a deep breath, would race across Chester Road into Victoria Street and Pierce Street, to see who could get farthest without another breath; code of honour prevented cheating.

"It wasn't sensible to arrive late for school and the daily examination of shoes and finger nails; slippers – or pumps – were still in use then.

"How well I remember sitting in Miss Williamson's class, learning letters and numbers. She always seemed a gentle soul to me and so unlike Alice Fountain, who, although scrupulously fair, was a strict disciplinarian; I know she always made me sit up straight.

"Mr Lea was the headmaster but I best remember Mr Worthington, who first unlocked my love of literature with Abou Ben Adhem and other poems.

"In those days, the side streets were almost devoid of motor traffic. On the main roads the red North Western, Leyland double-deckers, with their animal names like Tiger and Leopard, trundled off to Manchester. An occasional steam lorry or roller would disturb the peace and the Railway lorries with their three-wheel articulated cabs were to be seen delivering but it was hard to be run over.

"It was Down't Lane we first learned to bowl a decent length at cricket. Either that or spend ages in the long grass trying to find the corkie. It was a good place to practise cover drives too, for similar reasons. An old oil drum for wickets, a bat and handle to measure the crease and we played three bat-handles if a dismissal was doubtful. Oh yes – and keep yer eyes on't ball, it can bounce any road on these cinders – pads were unknown!

"Here also, we began to test ourselves against difficult trees, high walls and the final test of skill, the shirt-mill roof. We were certainly not angels but I cannot remember one incident of wilful damage to anybody's property and if we had to finally fight to settle an argument, whatever the result, the matter ended there.

"Chester Road and The Grove (that area at the bottom of Chestergate) had many businesses. Going down from 32, the first – apart from my Grandfather Goodwin who had his own cottage industry making pickles – was Mr Costello, the cabinet maker. From him I got sawdust for my rabbits and helped him with simple tasks but was not allowed home until I had properly cleared away any mess.

"Then came Mr Kirkham. A solidly-built old man with the empire builder's moustache so popular in those days and bristly white hair. He regularly indulged in the common pastime of doorstepping. Standing for ages with his pipe clenched; missing nowt. He was a rat catcher amongst other things. Grandfather told me he had a sideline docking puppies tails – with his teeth!

"Barker's decorator's shop was on the corner of Anderson Street and farther down were the Co-op butchers and grocers. A visit to the grocers often resulted in being given an Ovaltine tablet and where, if the shop was busy, a lady would be politely offered a chair while waiting. From here we got our iron hoops for bowling. We used to stand at the top of Hall Street and send them hurtling towards Longacre Street and St Alban's playground. They bounced and careered wildly over the sets and whoever was on guard at the bottom of the hill had to look sharp, or he'd get his shins barked; or something worse.

"On the other side of Chester Road, below Victoria Street, lived the Mottersheads and Jim Sutton, who kept pigeons. Then Archer's cake shop, the Dents and Stanley Sheldon's butcher's shop where we bought our meat and got ribs for clappers and a piece of sweet suet for chewing. Sheldons latterly became Arthur Carter's.

"Then came the Grove Hotel and it was here, when I was much older, the landlady – whose name I have shamefully forgotten – in the absence of a piano at home, used to let me practise in the back lounge.

"On the corner of Prestbury Road and King Edward Street was Neckwear's mill and on the corner of Prestbury Road and Chester Road the Butcher's Arms. Further along Prestbury Road, where it joined Longacre Street, was Berry's builder's yard. They had a black and white collie which had a habit of nipping you just when you thought it was friendly and docile.

"Those who know Chester Road now, may find it hard to believe we played top and whip on the pavement and 'mibs' in the gutters after school. The grids used to be a hazard though and there was no way but to lever them up and fish in the black slime at the bottom if a prized blood-alley found its way down.

"Those early years were carefree for most of us, but we sensed something was wrong when our fathers began to disappear to war. Although we didn't fully understand the enormity of what was happening, we knew it wasn't pleasant but we were protected from the real horrors by our families: then the Yanks arrived and things would never be the same again, for any of us.

"We used to sneak across the workhouse field to one of their camps, which was behind what became Miss Corin's school on Chester Road. They were very friendly and I suspect they looked on us as surrogates for their own children, for so many GI's would never see their own again. They always had the legendary gum and chocolates but we had to be careful, as did the soldiers, to avoid the wrath of the MPs, as we sneaked into the camp.

Frost's, Park Green, football team, 1938: the picture includes Joe Arnold, Cyril Davies, Jack Cross, Bill Shields, Guy Rose.

"Then as suddenly as they had arrived they disappeared to their embarkation points, leaving for many a void which took a long time to fill and which for some never was.

"There were plenty of characters about but there were two I remember in particular. Both were what you have today to call vertically challenged, a description which would have had them both rolling about with mirth.

"One was little Joey Barclay who was the air-raid warden for our area. He had his headquarters in the cellar of 34 Chester Road where the nuns lived and we kids would often sit with him and have a sip of tea. He was big hearted and kind and absolutely devoted to his duties.

"The other was Miss Polly Simpson. She too was very tiny and I remember her striding up and down Chester Road but never on the footpath, I think the kerbs were a problem for her. She spent her life helping others and I believe was awarded a medal by the Queen; no one could have done more to deserve it.

"As I grew up, I spent more time helping in the family shop in Park Lane. Eventually I was able to earn my pocket money by delivering orders on the big shop bike on which we had to carry boxes of vegetables and fruit in the pannier on the front. Toiling up Park Lane and Ryles Park Road with a full order was no joke, especially in winter. In 1947 the winter weather was so bad for so long, it was almost impossible to ride anywhere.

"Great-grandfather George had made it the policy of the shop to sell high class goods with the best possible service and this was continued down to my father. I have a lovely letter from Cyril Heapy who was errand boy for grandfather between 1925 and 1931. He says, "In those days we only dealt with the nobility and nobs and if someone rang to complain they had even one bad potato, I had to go as far as Prestbury with a replacement, such service guaranteed customer satisfaction.

"As we got older, we travelled farther afield for our excitement. We went conkering up Victoria Road and at the three lovely trees in the field between the hospital and the cricket ground. In those days the pond in the cemetery was full and was always a lure. We played football on the areas below the bandstand in the park and spent hours in the museum – under the watchful eye of the attendant – looking at the tiger, panda and all the old Egyptian relics.

"Once, it was possible to get from Hope Street West to Beck's Lane and only cross one road. We went through the workhouse field, along the back of Eiflanders estate, along the cricket ground and across Victoria Road into Fox's nursery, which was opposite Parkside and so across the fields to Upton and Beck's fields and lane. Beck's fields – where Upton Priory estate is now – was a regular picnic spot for families. On their weekend walks they would come from town, along Prestbury Road, through the fields and return along Priory Lane and Victoria Road.

"I remember one incident, concerning the rooks, which used to nest in hundreds, in the stand of trees in the grounds of Grangelands, at the Prestbury Road end of Beck's Lane. The mess and noise they made was dreadful. So the Fire Service came with their hoses and as a practice, hosed all the nests our before the birds could breed. It was certainly effective but unlikely ever to be repeated today.

A familiar shop in the town centre around the Second World War ... Lucille's in Derby Street (now Churchill Way).

"After the war many things began to change. In particular our old stamping ground the workhouse fields suddenly became taboo. Half of it was fenced off for hay crops and the top was left for grazing. There used to be a white horse which we were sure was possessed. As we still tried to use our usual route to the other fields, we paid careful attention to the whereabouts of the horse. Then when we felt it was safe, off we would go but that horse was clever. It would wait until we had reached the point of no return and then come charging across the fields and on at least one day, high-jump records were created, as we sailed over the barbed-wire fence. The horse would stamp and rake the ground, its eyes blazing with fury when it realised we were safe.

"Apart from the outdoor life, as with most youngsters, the cinemas were a constant draw. It was, however, essential that we were properly fuelled for the excitement and anxiety, which were part of the adventures of The Bowery Boys, Johnny Mack Brown and of course The Lone Ranger. So it was we stocked up on the way with – once rationing was over – sherbet dips, Pontefract cakes and the ever-present liquorice sticks. On the way home we would call in the shop on the corner of Water Street and Roe Street for a penny mineral. These were made by adding water to the relevant crystals and shaking the bottle with vigour, if you wanted to take the bottle out you had to pay another penny deposit.

"As we got older and were allowed to go to first house pictures, as soon as the show was over we made a bee-line for Belfield's chippie on Chestergate for tripe and chips and bread and butter, although for some of the lads Mrs Belfield's fair daughter, Sheila, was an added attraction.

"Saturday morning was always swimming time. We would be at the baths before they opened at eight, to be first to dive in but we had to wait while Mr Booth or the attendant 'scummed' the water. We always left in order to watch the nine o'clock London express steam through Central Station then off we would dash to the little shop in Roe Street, just by The Large Sunday School, for a fresh oatcake, which we ate on the way home.

"Sparrow Park and Brunswick Hill were favourite spots for train spotting and we would climb the wall at the Gas Road bridge and put old pennies on the railway line, for the engines to flatten.

"On reflection, we were on occasion foolhardy in our quest for excitement and it was probably as well our parents did not always know what we were up to. What we would never do though, would be to cause them shame or embarrassment – words which seem to have slipped out of today's vocabulary – for us that was a simple matter of conscience and right over wrong.

"When the time came for me to go to Kings', new horizons, friends and activities arrived too and although many of the activities remain largely unchanged I wonder how many re-member with affection the times in the 'fives court', demolished long ago and the wonderfully quirky end of year soirées; they, too, are no more I understand.

"We had great masters. A.A. Arnold known to all as 'A cubed', W. 'Slogger' Logan who was skilful with a gym shoe, Len Harvey and Selwyn Jones – who remains a dear friend to this day – all these gave of their time for hours after school for rugby, cricket and other activities. D.H. Burt who furthered my insatiable appetite for literature, Tommy Owen, the spherical maths master and so many more, all under the head T.T. Shaw. Work hard and play hard was a good description of those days but there was much humour and respect involved on both sides of the masters' desks.

"In those years of the late forties and early fifties, King George was still on the throne of England, Bill Hayley had yet to materialise and Jimmy Young was a crooner but there was plenty of music around.

"My father, who was drummer with the Paragon Dance Band, passed on to me his love of music in all its forms and soon after leaving school I, together with Norman 'Bronc' Read and other members from the old Paragon band, helped to form Macclesfield Jazz Club. The resident band, at the Stanley Hall, was The Silktown Stompers and of course visiting bands were booked; the most notable being The Merseysippi Jazz Band, which is still going strong today. That was a memorable night but unfortunately rock and roll was around the corner and public support was not enough to keep the club going. It was as they say though, great while it lasted.

"The other half of the 'we' I keep mentioning is my cousin and lifelong friend, Derek Wild. Together on our home-built bikes we had no horizons. Wincle was our second home, for rock climbing on the Hanging Rock, Indian Rock, Castle Rocks and Lud Church. We went swimming wherever there was water deep enough – Little Birtles Pool was a favourite. We went caving at Alderley and had tea and toast in the Wizard long before it was modernised.

"We had no television, only the wireless and wind-up gramophones, with 78 RPM records. We went dancing at Betty Jackson's, the Town Hall, the Stanley Hall, the Paroch' and the

40

dance studios at the bottom of Chestergate, above Jim Mottershead's cobblers shop and Hanson and Reece's. We also had the use of the piano, our bikes, friends and our own initiative and we were happy."

Dancing at the Stanley Hall – a Rotary Club dance in the 1950s. Guests are around the Tombola Stall.

It is a way of life irretrievably lost and one which did not prepare us for the second half of the century, when the world lost its way ethically. Years during which moral standards have drastically deteriorated and towns have been desecrated rather than resurrected.

Yet the true history of Macclesfield is founded on its people, who built it and developed it as the wonderful town it was. Their memories can never be dulled or their legacies erased.

41

10

Jack the Lad

Macclesfield will always remember Jack Sutton. Jack was a son of Macclesfield and, before he died, he was responsible for starting the ball rolling to purchase the costly Scanner for Macclesfield Hospitals. The Scanner Appeal, as it became known, was sub-titled the Jack Sutton Scanner Appeal. Thanks, Jack, from everyone who has had cause to use the Scanner and who will have cause to use it. Here's looking at you!

Jack's first job was as a butcher's boy at Charley Watson's butcher's shop in Stanley Street in 1934. The handyman at the shop at that time was Bill Bayley and he lived in Newgate. Charley Watson who had the family butcher's business at 7 Stanley Street was a prominent member of the Conservative Club and before that the Stanley Street premises used to be Goddard's meat and potato pie shop. In the year 1934, prime brisket was 4d a lb, that's about two new pence or less; prime pork was 11d, just under 5p. You could buy chilled beef for 4d a lb and there was the 1/6d 'lot' that comprised of a large rabbit, imported from China, one lb of beef or mutton and a lb of carrots.

I became a friend (I hope) of Jack's before his untimely death and he told me of the never-to-be-forgotten Saturday nights when, because there were no facilities for freezing in those days, everything had to be sold off. The shop would stay open until 11 p.m. when there would be queues of people waiting to buy the meat in lots of threepence or a tanner. They were mainly resident of the many boarding or doss houses that abounded around Stanley Street. Charley always referred to these people as 'July Bods' but for what reason Jack was never able to ascertain.

Taken outside the Lord Byron pub on July 10th, 1934, before an outing. Mrs Gertrude Timms was the licensee owner. On the second row is Polly Kendrick and the man at the back in the doorway was later her husband, Fred Pyatt. Gerty Timms is stood in the doorway (with large hat). Picture: Mr and Mrs Holland.

Young Jack Sutton first had the taste for hard work at a very early age when, as a young lad in the 1920s, his uncle, Jack Hammersley, had an oatcake and baker's business in Spital-fields where the car park to Sainsbury's first supermarket was. It then became T.J. Hughes' store. Uncle Jack was also the caretaker of the Sunday School and young Jack's job was to go out at five in the morning shouting "Oatcakes". He would come back with an empty basket and a pocket of money and would run up to Bond Street where Eddie Williamson had a post office and newsagents. He would collect a paper sack and run down to the station to pick up the papers from the train and be back at Bond Street by 6 a.m. to deliver them. Friday morning was a bit different for then the paper lads would be driven down in Eddie's car because there was an extra delivery that day – the Macclesfield Times was out at lunchtime and they had to be seen to. Then it was off to school at St Alban's and a paper round at night as well – all for five shillings which he gave to his mum and he would be given a bag of sweets for his pay.

Young Jack then worked part-time for Old Mother Kirk who had the butcher's shop in Roe Street and on Sundays he would help to kill the pigs and other animals with a man called Freddie Grundy.

During this time he was a keen young boxer and he was with three other well known Macclesfield names – Joe Dixon, who fought for the Schoolboys' Championship, Ernie Foden and Jock McKay who were known as the Evergreen Midgets. Their fights were not in the roped rings we know today but there would be merely a ring of spectators who would push the lads back into the fray if they were knocked into the crowd. Jack went on to work full time at Stanley Street and when the war came he joined the Queen's Own Hussars. After demob he was offered the princely sum of ten bob a week (50 new pence) to work for the Stanley Street butcher and so went to V and E Plastics, firstly as despatch clerk and then chief inspector.

The company was then next to George Bryan's salesrooms in premises previously known to many Maxonians as the Bazaar.

One day Jack had an idea that set him on the road to world-wide fame and travel. He nipped across the road to Wellings builders, got a ballcock used for plumbing and put the PVC material inside, held it over a flame and to his delight he found a revolutionary method of manufacturing a football in one piece. This was patented and became the Frido football later to be endorsed by Stanley Mathews. A machine was developed and the idea sold to Germany, where most of the plastic balls were coming from, and then sold to 28 different countries. Travel all over the world became the norm for Jack and he recalls meeting many famous people. He stayed as the guest of the great Pele and became personal friend of many soccer greats including Denis Law and Bobby Charlton. Jack recalled Sir Stanley Mathews being embarrassed by the amount of money being paid for his endorsement of the product

– one penny each. Sir Stan asked that this fee be reduced by half!

Not a bad career for a Macc lad who once sold oatcakes at five in the morning.

Keith Yearsley brought me this photograph that will no doubt get the memory banks working ... it is of West Park bowlers including George Floy, Ernest Eaton, Fred Baron, Isaac Findlow and Clem Kirk.

11

Fritters on a Friday, Savoury Ducks on a Thursday ...

Nancy Hadfield-Brocklehurst's earliest memories are of sitting in her pram, in the year 1927, with a row of ju ju jellies across the pram apron and her sister, Joan, who was then seven years of age, pinching them from her. Her next memory was of sitting on the pavement in front of the family house at 86 Arbourhay Street when she was about three. She was rattling a few pennies in an empty tin of Snow Fine face cream and the lid flew off – the coins rolled down the gutter and into the grid. How she cried! And the pennies were quickly replaced.

Nancy has many more memories of those days around Arbourhay Street; days gone forever ... but remaining in our hearts.

In February of 1994 she was sitting on a beach while on holiday in Hikkaduwa, Sri Lanka. As she sat in the shade of a tree, looking out over the Indian Ocean, her thoughts went back to those times. This is part of what she wrote:

"I believe that at one time there were four chip shops in that area, two along Commercial Road, and two on Hurdsfield Road and it was the latter two which I knew. Apart from Mr and Mrs Pearson's there was Parker's. Mr Parker ran his shop with his son and his daughter, Winifred. By now Winifred was a beautiful teenager, with lovely face, flowing red wavy hair and a super figure. I so admired her and hoped very much I too would look like her one day, and even today when I meet Winifred, with her youth long gone, she is still a lovely woman, that aura about her still, and what's more so nice to know! I've told her of my admiration for her, she was very embarrassed!

"Now Pearson's chip shop was where I visited. The Pearsons were quite dedicated to their work; they had to do things right, their fish and chips tasted good. There was always a snaking queue , people would stand with basins under their arms – quite the norm in those days. They sold minerals; Cream-Soda was my favourite, Dandelion and Burdock, lemonade, Tizer and Vimto; these would be on display on a high shelf all round the shop – no cold cabinets for cool drinks. In the window on a huge willow plate was the tripe with a cut-out card which had UCP in large letters and underneath the opening hours of the shop, and another card 'Fritters on Friday's, Savoury Ducks on Thursday', and yet another card 'We Aim to Please'. The fryer was huge and took up the whole of the wall; it had a mirror in the middle, there were four big pans double-hinged with shiny aluminium lids that when opened filled the shop with steam. Mr Pearson ladled out the fish and chips while Mrs Pearson wrapped them up. She was kept so busy – all you would hear would be her asking "salt, vinegar?" She had no time for conversation, her hair was always damp on her forehead.

"In an alcove at the side was a flat-topped gas cooker that held four black iron pans with long straight handles. These held the steak and kidney puddings, suet and mushy peas. The best thing that happened in the shop was to watch the potatoes being cut, so I would squeeze into the corner near the large black-handled chipper. There were always two large enamel buckets, one holding the large white potatoes, and the other bucket to catch the chips. Sometimes it took several pulls on the handle to get the potato through, and the whole of the narrow counter with the white tiles would vibrate so much that the ancient looking salt pot (which was made of tin and was very large and battered as if it had been dropped a lot) would go dancing along the counter and bang into the vinegar bottle. Once this operation was over, off I would go, perhaps home to see what Mother was doing, or go and play in the park.

"A whole new world opened for me when I was seven. Up till

then I just played in Victoria Park, but when I became errand girl, well, I became very inquiring and found out I liked being with my elders, watching and listening to them. I didn't talk much, I know that for sure. Mother would say to me, "Nancy, keep out of the shop – you only go in when you are doing my errands!" But I had found a new entertainment, I did not heed her words because to my mind I had been a customer, and would be in the future, so what was wrong with visiting a shop when I had nothing to buy? I was in and out of shops like a rabbit out of a warren. Only Clara Malins seemed to mind, and even she didn't complain, well not to me anyway!

Airing the Aspidistras

"Apart from the weather (of course) you would know it was summer when front doors were opened. By this, I mean left open, some wide open, some just a crack, so if you walked by you would get a glimpse of dark brown sideboards with ornaments such as a cheery girl holding cherries to her mouth. We had a figurine of an Alsatian dog which I disliked very much, and I don't know why we had it, as a family we didn't care for dogs. We had cats. Anyhow, chairs and stools would be brought out and if they were old men they would have their pipes; the wives would put on a clean pinny, over their skirts or dresses, that usually went down to their ankles, thick lisle stockings and black laced shoes. They would enjoy being out for, after all, it was more pleasant to be sat at the front door, there were more people passing, more going on. Few had gardens at the back, most had communal yards they had to share. So it was much more pleasant at the front of the house. They would bring out the aspidistra plants at the end of a hot day knowing full well there would be a thunder storm. The old would say "Ay, we'll have a drop of rain toneet." More often than not they were right.

"I would enjoy going up and down the street saying 'hello' to everyone, for it was not every day that so many people were out at one time. And in the evening the men would go to the pub for a few drinks; it seemed to be only at weekends the wives joined them.

The 23rd St Andrew's Scouts pictured on Mayor's Sunday, November 9th, 1929. Seated, front row, left to right: Clifford Merriman, Harold Durrant, Victor Merriman, Victor Riseley, Fred Hulme, Clifford Poole, Norman Riseley (next six not known). Second row, seated: P.L. Ken Hilditch, P.L. Leslie Riseley, Mr John Riseley (president), cub master Louis Riseley, G.S.M. Adam Hope, Asst S.M. Albert Dobson, Mr Albert Wood (treasurer), Troop Leader Albert Wood, P.L. George Corbishley, P.L. Alan Knotley. Third row (standing): Billy Ban, ? Derbyshire, Bob Barker, Jim Hill, Dennis Sellers, not known, ? Forster, Syd Wood, Dick Dobson, not known, Jack Steel. Back row: Harvey Jones, John Dobson, Jack Vigrass, Joe Barker, not known, not known, Stan Webster, Jack Bann, Maurice Bann, Walter Barnes.

"This was a time in the late thirties when shawls were really going out of fashion, but I remember three old women who still wore them; one was a Mrs Parton. At the same time every night, with shawl round her head and shoulders and with a well concealed jug, she went to the pub, the 'Elephant and Castle', for her nightly stout; back she would come minutes later, looking neither left nor right, and straight into her house!

"Many times, I've heard my parents say people were content, there was more happiness, less competition, you settled for what you had without complaint and if people were poor, and they were, they still had their standards. Proof is the good families that were raised, more often than not on one wage. We never heard of muggings, we wouldn't have known what drugs were. I don't think there was much burglary going on. There was the odd policeman walking up and down or, if he was mobile, riding a bicycle."

It wasn't going to be too long before this way of life was to change with 1939 looming – change for everyone, everywhere.

We have already looked at two of the town's Silk Queens. The Carnival parade had many hundreds of local participants and was watched by thousands. Pictured is William Frost's Park Green Mill Jazz Band in 1932.

12

Delivery Boy

Geoffrey Hunter became a firm friend of mine after he called in to the Macclesfield Express office one day with a few sheets of paper in his hand.

"Are these any use?" he asked me, and handed me the beginning of what was to become a highly popular series of articles based on his childhood in the Waterloo Street area of Hurdsfield and entitled 'Waterloo Sunset', then 'Waterloo Boy'.

Now this 'Waterloo Boy' has – I'm very pleased to say – contributed to this latest volume of Macclesfield memories. In it he reminisces about his time as a delivery boy – the title he gives to it.

"Throughout the 1930s and up to the time of King George V's death in 1936 my family's life in the upper reaches of Waterloo Street was not greatly influenced by the run of shops which extended from lower Hurdsfield Road, through Gladstone Square and along Commercial Road to where Leah's Steam Bakery stood at the corner of Queen Street. While, through the years, incidental purchases were made by us along this 300 yards or so stretch, in the main it served merely as an animated backdrop to our lives since the little shops close by us and Buxton Road businesses supplied most of our needs.

"The move from Waterloo Street to Crew Avenue, although little more than a quarter of a mile in distance, changed our lives completely. It meant more than a change of house; we now had a change of grocer, greengrocer, butcher, baker, chip-shop, newsagent and hairdresser as this busy thoroughfare became more meaningful to us. And with change came choice also, for

51

most types of businesses were either duplicated, triplicated and even quadrupled, come to think of it, when I recall the butchers Rowbotham, Cooperative Society, Taylor and Kirk.

Commercial Road showing what was Rutters' Shop in the 1930s. (G. Pownall)

"At the time of our move my elder brothers Tony and Vincent were of an age to participate in part-time jobs and during the next two years each was employed either as paper boy by Mr & Mrs Jack Nield at the corner of Blagg Street or as delivery boy by greengrocer Mr Jack Hopwood and his wife a few yards further up the road. In 1938, or thereabouts, the Hopwoods sold their business to Mrs Florrie Wright in order to pursue a similar venture in Chester Road. As was customary and sensible, Mrs Wright and the Hopwoods ran the Hurdsfield shop together for some weeks as part of the transaction and during this period Mrs Wright developed a great fondness for Vincent, the Hopwood's delivery boy at that time, and was greatly saddened when he elected to move to Chester Road with them following the change-over.

"At this point I stepped into the breach to save the day. I was just 11 years old and it was my first part-time job. Mrs Wright was a lovely lady. She was of the Avery family of Langley and previously had been widowed a young Mrs Birchenough with a little boy, Joe. Tragedy had followed tragedy and later she had lost the young, angelic Joe as well but her faith had stood her in good stead. Her second husband, George, was employed by Macclesfield Corporation. He tended to be rather reserved, probably due to a sight weakness, for his spectacles had very thick lenses and I likened them – without humour, you understand – to bottle bottoms. In the course of time I found him to be just as kind and gentle as his wife who, incidentally, was assisted in the shop by her sister Miss Elsie Avery who came regularly from Langley.

"Precisely what my duties were supposed to be from the outset, or what wages I received, does not readily come to mind. For one thing, I seemed to become a member of the family immediately and although Fridays after school and all-day Saturday duties were obligatory, I would pop in after school on other days and assist on a regular basis. Remuneration was not a big issue either since I was totally devoid of mercenary intent and happily handed over to my mother whatever coinage came my way, probably in the region of two shillings and sixpence per week.

"As shops go, Mrs Wright's was quite sizeable. The floor was slightly higher than the outside pavement so the doorway had a step and the shop counter was on the right as one entered, running at a right-angle to the road. Behind the door there were two or three feet of space to the back wall. A deep shelf, partitioned into sections and at adult waist height sloped gently forward on stout wooden legs and contained the bulk of the fruit for sale. Underneath, light from the glass panelled door fell upon a crate of sterilized milk and a large set of see-saw scales with a generous scoop dish and a supporting cast of weights. Two substantial wooden potato containers which tapered downwards to the stone-flagged floor came next followed by various open boxes and open-necked sacks. These, containing mainly vegetables, jostled for space to catch the eye.

"One tastefully-lined box would contain fresh diced vegetables, the price-ticket describing the assortment as 'pot herbs', an ideal mixture for soups and stews. Finally, tucked away in the far corner close by the door leading to the back of the shop was a case or two of the new household bleach, 'Lanry', a name coined from the Christian names of the producers, Alan and Harry Brown. Above this array were shelves containing tinned foods and dried goods to which customers could help themselves and transfer to the counter.

"Given decent weather (and we seemed to get more of it in those days), goods would be displayed outside the shop. It was not unusual for such shops to have a narrow board hinged to the window-sill with a supporting chain at each end which could be lowered to form a shelf for this purpose. Cabbage, cauliflower etc, and punnets of strawberries in the summer would advertise themselves in this way.

"I was a Central School boy at the time and greatly influenced by the art master, Mr Brocklehurst. His was one of the few classes in which I showed any aptitude. My talent was quickly utilized by Mrs Wright and to my duties was added that of ticket-writer. I was into 'shadow writing' in those days (my own description), which was a fragmented and illusory form of writing which fascinated my employer and undoubtedly elevated me in her estimation.

"Pricing of goods had to be calculated and monitored carefully, for 15 yards up the road Mr & Mrs Fred Worth had a similar business. A ticket ploy failed to work for us on one occasion. Following instructions, I produced a potato ticket which read 'King Edward's, 7lbs for 6d'. No sooner was the ticket in place when into the shop came an eagle-eyed middle-aged woman. Glancing critically at my most recent art creation, she commented, "King Edward's, seven pounds for sixpence? I'm not paying that. I can get 'em at Fred Worth's for a penny a pound!" And out of the shop she stormed ...

"Mid-week, I was always available for the weighing of produce and the spontaneous delivery of orders. 'Would you like the boy to deliver them to you?' was a question often asked of customers, but my Friday and Saturday duties were more premeditated. On Fridays, after school, I would collect my note-book from the shop and stroll leisurely around the area collecting orders for delivery the next day. I was glad to be introduced to the job during a period of light nights for one of my calls was to the vicarage adjoining Hurdsfield Church. The Rev Isaac Hutchinson's home was, like the church, old and set well back from the road and I had to flirt briefly with the grave-stones to reach it. I think a dark baptism to that duty would have scared the life out of me!

King Edwards were seven pounds for a tanner. (G. Hunter)

"Come Saturday, I would bring out the cart from the back of the shop – a shallow wooden box with a pair of push-chair wheels and shaft handles – and delivery would commence. My first delivery of an order to Mrs Hutchinson at Hurdsfield

Vicarage has stayed in my memory ever since. Having paid me the required sum for her order Mrs H. proffered a penny tip. No, thank you very much, I said. She was clearly surprised and puzzled by my refusal and tried again, but I was adamant. I could not bring myself to explain that I regarded her money as holy – God's money, in fact – and I was unworthy of it. From that point until my delivery the next week this lady must have given the matter much thought for having paid for her second order she produced a money-box. "Would you like to take this home with you?" she asked. "It's a Church Missionary box and at any time you have a copper to spare you can put it in the box, and in due course it will do a lot of good. Here, there's a penny tip for you to start the ball rolling ... " and she dropped the coin through the slot and each week afterwards would tip me with a penny and say "... and that's for your box." What a clever and perceptive lady she was! The box was given a set spot on the sideboard at home for use by all the family and was returned filled at a later date.

"Of course, I still remember many of the families I visited, even though it is more than 50 years ago. A Saturday morning call would be to the Kay residence, the first house on the left in Fence Avenue. Mr Kay had a business at Lower Heys, his wife was a staunch supporter of the Girl Guide and Brownie movement and they had a son, Stanley and a daughter, June. I called also at the Francis home in Brocklehurst Avenue, opposite Hurdsfield House. Mr Francis was chemistry master at my school and he and his wife had two daughters, the youngest of whom, Margaret, developed into a superb athlete and became British Sprint Champion and a top international before becoming a doctor.

"The Gortons in Queens Avenue were also on my round as also were the Clarkes a little further along on the other side. Mr Gorton was a renowned french-polisher. His wife was a petite and most attractive lady. They had young lads, Alan and Stanley, and little daughter, Marjorie, who today lives at Weston, Stafford. The Clarkes, I believe I am right in saying, had close connections with the Royal Oak public house which stood back from the road in Gladstone Square.

"In Hawthorn Way, I recall the Potts family on the left as the road came to an end. Their two little girls were like fairy tale princesses and, young lad though I was, I also took note of the dark, mature beauty of Olga of the Compton (or was it Compston?) family when I called on them in the crescent of Nicholson Avenue as it swept round the top before descending hurriedly to form the junction with Brocklehurst Avenue. Yes indeed, I remember them all so well ...

"Sadly, Mrs Wright never savoured in the shop the contentment she had sought and after I had been with her for about two years she decided to call it a day and retire gracefully with George to their cottage higher up Hurdsfield Road. Her shop became Ferris's shoe repairers. Her retirement meant a door had closed for me also but, as is often the case in life, another door opened for me shortly afterwards.

"Perhaps, on another occasion when my pen becomes restless and in need of exercise, it will tell you that story as well."

Beaconsfield Conservative Club, Arbourhay Street, before it was demolished. Most of the houses in this street were one up and one down plus a kitchen and a bed could be put at the top of the stairs. The walls were, at least in the thirties and forties, mainly whitewashed. They were cosy homes full of warmth from the people and from the coal fire. (G. Pownall)

57

13

Wrapped in Brown Paper and Tied with String

Denis Bamford was born in 1928 at Fern Lea, Saville Street, Macclesfield. His parents were Winifred and Samuel Bamford. Later, Denis emigrated to South Australia but still keeps in touch with his family in Macclesfield and, I am pleased to say, keeps in touch with me.

He wrote to me in early 1994 recalling shops and shopping during the period of the 1930s to the 1950s. He also recalled local schools of that time.

Here are his recollections:

"To begin with, most of the shops were 'corner shops', even if they were not always on the corner of the street. Most of the shops would be privately owned and operated by one family; usually dad went out to work, while mum ran the shop and looked after the kids. One or two of the larger family shops would be more organised, with perhaps members of the family working in the shop, or even a couple of paid staff. The nearest one got to a large company operating in Macclesfield was the M.E.P.S. (Macclesfield Equitable and Provident Society) also known at various times as the C.W.S. (Co-operative Wholesale Society) – or the Co-op, or sometimes referred to as the 'Stores'. They had a number of branches around the town and the ones that come immediately to mind were located in Bank Street, two on Buxton Road, Park Lane, and of course, the main complex on Park Green.

Billy Johnson was a professional league footballer who was brought to Macclesfield by Mr Bayley. He later had this shop in Mill Lane where he is pictured.

"The 'Stores' we patronised was in Bank Street. Most of the goods were packaged differently in those days – this was long before the arrival of pre-packaged goods. For instance, cheese would be displayed on the counter, in the round, as it came from the dairy, and this would be cut and wrapped as required by each customer. Bacon would be on display by the whole side and this would be removed from the hook and sliced on the machine, even if you only wanted a couple of rashers. Sugar, rice and dried peas etc would be taken from the storage bins by the scoop, weighed and packaged while you waited. Sugar was always placed in a stiff, blue paper bag and tied up with a good quality, fine string which was always referred to as sugar string. This string was always saved as it was such good quality and used around the house. Tea was always sold by the quarter or half pound packet. Coffee was always bottled coffee, usually 'Camp Coffee, with Chicory'. There were always tangerines available, just before Christmas, but this stopped with the beginning of World War II.

"The weekly shopping was always done at the Bank Street Stores and the assistants waited upon each customer personally. The assistants were mathematical geniuses, totting up long columns of figures with nothing more complicated than a sharp pencil and a piece of paper. Of course the prices would have farthings, half-pennies, or even three farthings attached to the pence column, just to make the addition a little more complicated. If the order was not too big, it would be wrapped up in brown or white paper, tied up with string and the customer would take their groceries with them. If it was a large order, it would be placed in a cardboard box and put on one side until the delivery boy came after school, and he would deliver the parcel either by handcart or by delivery bicycle.

"One thing that used to amaze me, particularly in the grocery shops, was the dexterity of the assistants when it came to parcelling up the groceries. A parcel of weekly provisions would be assembled, and then came the tricky bit, wrapping it up in a sheet of brown paper, and tying it up with string. The assistant would pull on the end of the string from a metal string dispenser, and then tie the parcel up so the string went 'north to south and east to west'. Then by some means I have never been able to fathom out, they were able to create some kind of slip knot, pull the string up tight and then cut the string away from its container. This way they never wasted any string. All this was accomplished with a flourish and a certain amount of showmanship, and some assistants, just to show their confidence in their abilities, would give the string a smart twang, just to show it was taut and secure. I still can't tie a parcel up using this method, I have to create the slip knot first and that can get me into all kinds of trouble.

"One of the attractions of shopping at the Co-op was that it offered 'the divi', or a dividend on all the money you spent. Say for every pound sterling you spent, you would be credited with say twopence or whatever the rate was. This meant when you paid for your groceries or any other purchase, and you were a registered member of the Co-op, you would give the shop assistant your check number, which was your membership number. The assistant would record your check number – in our case 1004 – and the amount you had spent on a receipt. You kept the top copy and the carbon copies were sent to head office, where they were credited to your account. Once or twice a year you could go to the 'Co-op Bank' on Park Green and have your dividend either paid into your account, or paid over the counter in cash.

Smaller shops in the neighbourhood

"The smaller corner shops also provided a valuable service to the neighbourhood in many ways. The nearest shop was Jackson's chippy, as we called it. Jackson's Chip Shop, to give it its full title, was located in Copper Street, almost opposite the northern end of Saville Street. They provided wholesome supplies of fried fish, chips and boiled peas, which made many a mid-week lunch for a lot of people. Jacksons also supplied cow-heel and tripe and savoury ducks. Today's operators would be staggered at the amount of hard labour that went into producing fish and chips. I think the Jackson's may have had a machine to clean the potatoes, but they still had to be checked and the eyes removed before they could be used. The potatoes were turned into chips one potato at a time. The chipping machine was mounted on the counter, and in the base of the machine were a series of blades arranged in quarter inch squares. The potato was placed end up on these blades and then a counter-balanced arm was pulled to bring down a cast iron block, which pushed the potato through the blades, producing chips that were approximately quarter of an inch square, and the length of the potato. The cast iron block was made in such a way to fit into the top of the blades so that they were not damaged. Once the operator let go of the handle the heavy block would rise and return to the rest position, ready for the next potato. Sometimes, if the potatoes were a little tough or on the large size, it would take Mr Jackson a couple of attempts to get the potatoes through the chipper, it was then that the whole counter would quiver and shake, but the counter never collapsed. For some strange reason, when the shop was not operating as a fish and chip shop, Mr Jackson, or Bobby Jackson as he was known, because he was a Special Constable, operated a butcher's shop from the same counter. The meat was always good quality, but supplies dwindled with the onset of rationing at the beginning of World War II. Mrs Jackson and her daughter Lex, ran the chip shop side of the business.

"Around the corner in Black Road, almost back to back with Jacksons, was Mrs Belfield's small shop, it was so small that about three people waiting to be served would crowd out the shop space. Yet Mrs Belfield, or Grandma Belfield as she was known, managed to eke out a living selling small amounts of groceries, sweets, biscuits and odds and ends. At that time you could buy 2oz of sweets or a small bar of chocolate for a penny or twopence, so she wouldn't have many large transactions in her daily sales.

"Further along Black Road, on the corner of Bradley Street, was Pickford's shop. They had what appeared to be a large variety of stock that seemed to go from floor to ceiling. I don't think there was a square inch of space that wasn't used. The shop was run by Mr and Mrs Pickford, and I seem to recall Mrs Pickford as always being a well-dressed, quiet lady.

Mrs Sheila Hall of Larch Avenue read my last book and saw that her parents' chip shop at 101 Chestergate was mentioned. She kindly sent me this photograph of the shop about 1949-50 and wrote: "It will bring back a lot of memories because there are still many people who remember and talk to me about 'your chippie'. After all, it was about 40 years since we left there!

Mrs May Belfield seen with daughter Sheila 'on duty' in 1950 (photo supplied by Mrs Sheila Hall). Sheila, 17 years old on this photograph, was born at the shop but earlier her parents kept a chippie in Commercial Road, just round the corner from the bottom of Fence Street. She recalls that during the war American soldiers were very good customers and a number were billeted near the shop. Her mother regularly cooked large batches of 'french fries' and these were greatly appreciated by the Americans, who placed very large orders. The shop was also a favourite for patrons of The Picturedrome.

"A few doors along there was a small butcher's shop, but apart from it being there, I can't recall much about it or its owners.

"On the corner of Black Road and Windmill Street was Cundliffs. (I'm not certain if this is the correct spelling.) Cundliffs was the local Post Office and general store, again with a very small floor space. There were two counters, one for general groceries and the like, the other was purely for postal business. Mr Cundliff ran the post office, I recall him as being a stiff, little man with a close cropped moustache; his wife was in charge of the other side of the business, but often their roles would be interchanged. Again the daily takings could not have been large, but somehow or other they managed to make a living.

"The next shop was on the corner of Copper Street and

Windmill Street. I can't recall the name of the owners, but it did seem rather bleak and austere and poorly stocked.

"Next door but one, going down Windmill Street, from Copper Street, was the newsagents, Harry Turner. Harry Turner usually had a few comics on display in his window but hardly carried any stock in his shop.

"His stock was here today and gone tomorrow. Harry used to deliver the daily and weekly papers and magazines to homes in the neighbourhood, come hail, rain or shine. Then he would call on a Saturday morning to collect the money for the week's papers.

"There is one shop in the neighbourhood I have not mentioned, because it was not strictly a shop. I refer to Stan Furness, the barber (or men's hairdresser). Stan's place was located in Copper Street, directly opposite to the entrance of the dye-works of John Abraham and Son. In those days it cost four pence to get your hair cut during the week days and sixpence on Saturdays. You could have your hair cut however you liked as long as it was short back and sides with a bit off the top. A shave was extra. The business took place in the front room, facing Copper Street, there was a wooden bench that would hold about six people, one barber's chair, a marble wash stand with an ancient gas geyser which provided the hot water for shaves, and there was a large mirror over the fire place. The fire place was always blocked off with a large cardboard advert for Lux toilet soap. The sign was in two pieces and one piece usually overlapped the other, so the words then read 'Lux Toilet Soap'. Stan Furness, when I knew him, was a grey-haired, sallow complexioned man. He always seemed to wear a tatty black waistcoat which was invariably covered in hair clippings and cigarette ash. The other piece of equipment in his shop, I'd almost forgotten about. It was his tandem bicycle. Stan and his wife were reputed to be keen cyclists in their day, ranging far and wide. I can't remember actually seeing the tandem outside the shop, and one didn't see much of Mrs Furness either. But that's where I used to get my hair cut as a child, and so did half the neighbourhood. Stan must have had some skill as a barber for later, during World War II, he spent a lot of time in his profession at the RAF Camp in Wilmslow. I've no idea what kind of equipment was used at the RAF Camp, but in his own business at that time I never knew Stan to use anything more sophisticated than a pair of hand shears. He actually had two pairs, one for rough cutting and another pair for fine work. Both pairs had the trick of pulling at your hair as he clipped away at the back of your head. When Stan saw you grimace he would stop and ask: "Does it hurt?", and if he thought you were playing up he would continue: "Funny, I didn't feel it." He would then walk away from the chair, brush the teeth of the clippers with a fine brush, add a spot of oil to the mechanism and then it was back to work. When he had finished the haircut he would always spray one's hair with a liquid from a fine mist spray. I think it was a mixture of something called Bay Rum and water, and it was used to keep your hair in place at least until one got outside the shop door. Stan used to kid the children and tell them it was his special 'cut and come again' liquid, so that their hair would grow and they would have to return a few weeks later for another haircut.

Macclesfield town shops

"One shop that must rate a mention before looking at other shops in Macclesfield is one that was used by thousands of people, and that is Bowers' Chemist at the bottom of Windmill Street, in fact it was known as Bowers Corner. It had a cornucopia of supplies from medicine of all kinds through to what was known as dry salt goods. Mr Bowers must have filed thousands of prescriptions over the years, and literally helped untold numbers of people. He was assisted by his daughter and I think his other main assistant was a man called Mr Rigby.

"Once one got into Macclesfield town centre, the shops were bigger and more sophisticated, one or two would be nationally, or even internationally owned, but largely they were owned and operated by local families.

"I suppose the best-known international establishment was F.W. Woolworth & Company, always known just as Wool-worths. In my young days it was known and advertised as the 'Threepenny and Sixpenny store'. Nothing would cost more than threepence or sixpence, was their proud boast. Many, many items cost a lot more than sixpence, but to meet their advertising claims they would break their items up into several components. For example, an electric table lamp would be sold:

The lamp itself	6d
Electric wire flex	6d
Three-pin plug	6d
Shade	6d
60w bulb	3d
Total	2/3d

– and this style of business seemed to work, for there never appeared to be any shortage of customers.

Today, an extension has been built on to the side of the Town Hall in Macclesfield. A number of buildings were pulled down in the forties and part of the Market moved onto the site of the Union Gateway and the Unicorn Gateway. This picture was taken in the 1950s and shows the area before the 'Nun's Hats' market stalls were erected.

"Another store which seemed to have a similar business phi-losophy, in that you could buy things in small quantities, was

67

Halford's cycle and later motor parts dealer on the corner of Exchange Street and Mill Street, I think that they too had branches throughout the North-West of England.

"The Maypole, located on the other side of Mill Street, was one of a national chain of retail grocers. One of their sale presentations, apart from a spotlessly clean shop, was the presentation of butter. In those days the butter was delivered to the shops in huge blocks, which had to be cut up and weighed into individual portions and the Maypole employed men especially to do this. They were known as butter slappers. They would take the huge block of butter, cut it, weigh it, knock it into a presentable shape, roughly the size of the prepackaged block we know today, and then with a final flourish they would slap the top face of the butter pack with a wooden paddle on which was engraved a pattern, such as a cow or a rose, and then the butter was ready for presentation to the customer. Alas these skills died with the outbreak of World War II, and rationing.

"George Mason's, the grocers, was a little lower down Mill Street from Queen Victoria Street. This was an interesting shop in that it had an aerial transportation system to handle the cash transactions. After making your purchase and paying the assistant, he or she would place your money and account into a container, hook in onto an overhead tramway, suspended from the ceiling, then pull a lever. The container and your money then would zoom across the shop, over the heads of the shoppers, to an office at the back of the shop. Here, the cashier would remove the money and account, check it, and then place the receipt and change and send it speeding back to the assistant, who by this time had parcelled up your purchases. There was only one other shop in town, that I can recall, which used this method of handling cash, and that was Holland and Barwood (Drapers) in Chestergate. But it was always George Mason's shop that drew the attention of the kids and they would stand fascinated and open mouthed as the cash containers flew backwards and forwards across the shop.

"A shop I used to pass regularly and one that provided a great deal of delight and speculation for all youngsters, was Bayley's Toy Shop. Bayley's was located on Mill Lane, on the southern side of Lower Bank Street; it was a large double-fronted shop with a large undercover entrance between the two shop windows. Over the years Bayley's must have provided simply hundreds, if not thousands of bicycles, dolls, prams and all kinds of toys for the kids of Macclesfield. The window on the northern side of the shop always took my attention with a varied collection of model railway engines, model cars, toy soldiers, wooden forts, castles, cowboy and Indian outfits, six shooters and the like. The other window wasn't worth looking at as far as the boys were concerned, it was full of dolls, prams, tea-sets, dolls' houses and the like. No self-respecting lad would ever be caught looking at such rubbish. No doubt the girls thought the same about 'our' window.

"For most of the year, the arcade between the two shop fronts of Bayley's would have a few of the larger toys, or prams on display, but come December, Father Christmas was there. No matter how cold it was, how wet it was or how much snow there was, Father Christmas would be there, stamping up and down to keep warm. There was always time for a cheery word to the smallest child and time to call "Merry Christmas" to the passers-by. As we grew older we soon realised that it was only old Mr Bayley, dressed as Father Christmas, but there was a time when we thought it was really Father Christmas.

"In addition to being a very fit man, to be able to spend so many cold, cold hours outside his shop, dressed as Father Christmas, Mr Bayley senior must have been a very astute businessman, for he had the garage on the opposite side of the road, which also sold oil and petrol, car parts and bicycles. The emphasis changed somewhat through the lean years of World War II, when petrol was rationed and there were no cars for sale.

"Of course, there were many, many more shops in operation, but those I have mentioned come readily to mind. I wonder sometimes whether it would be worthwhile to sit down and list all the businesses I can remember, the only trouble would be to get them into some kind of order, but that's a job for another day.

HOLLAND & BARWOOD
SALE

STARTS TODAY, THURSDAY, JULY 19
where you can always be sure of QUALITY GOODS

Household Linens

CANDY STRIPED SHEETS
70 x 100 .... **38/-** pair
90 x 100 .... **48/-** pair

OSMAN SHEETS
70 x 100 ...... **35/11** pair
80 x 100 ...... **39/11** pair
90 x 100 ...... **45/11** pair

Candlewick BEDSPREADS
Single Size ...... **38/-** each
Double Size ... **52/-** each

ALL WOOL BLANKETS
Made by Moderna
60 x 80. Only ... **35/-** each

STRIPED BLANKET SHEETS
Single Size. Only ... **21/-**
(each)

COTTON DAMASK NAPKINS
Large Size ... **1/6** each
Special quality ... **1/11½**
(each)

TABLECLOTHS
36 x 36 Printed Floral Cloth
(each) **3/11½**
49 x 49 Seersucker Cloth
(each) **7/11**
50 x 50 Gaily Coloured Check
Cloth (each) **10/-**

Carpets and Furniture

SLUMERLAND SPRING INTERIOR MATTRESSES
3ft. **£7/19/0**
4ft. **£9/19/0**

FOAM MATTRESS
Covered—Ideal for caravans
(each) **95/-**

PILLOWS
Flock Stripe Ticks ... **8/11**
Feather—White Ticks Made
by Fogarty's **11/-**

HAIRCORD CARPET
1 only. 3 x 3½ ... **£12/0/0**

AXMINSTER RUGS
24 x 48 approx. **24/-**
33 x 66 approx. **44/-**
36 x 72 approx. **55/-**

AXMINSTER STAIR CARPET
18in. wide. (yd.) ... **15/11**

NUMDAH WOOL RUG
15/- ...... and **25/-**
6ft. 4in. (each) **44/-**

INDIAN SLIP MATS
(each) **15/-**

Towels

Hand Towel with multi-check
design (each) **3/11½**
Striped Hand Towel
(each) **4/11**

ZORBIT WHITE TOWEL
(slightly seconds)
22 x 44 (each) **4/11**
30 x 54 (each) **6/11**

BATH TOWELS (striped)
30 x 60 .... **10/-** each
Pastel Coloured:
30 x 60 .... **14/-** each
Reversible Patterned. Ideal
Beach Towel ... **21/-** each

PILLOWCASES
Plain Housewife (ea.) **2/11½**
Candy-Stripe **3/11½**
Scolloped and Hemstitched
(each) **5/11**
2-Row Cord **5/11**

PILLOW TICKS (White)
Feather Proof **4/6**
BOLSTER CASES
Full Size ...... **5/11** each

YELLOW POLISHERS
Large Size ...... **1/-** each
Extra Large ...... **1/6** each

Furniture Bargain

AVALON BEDROOM SUITE
Dressing Table, 4ft. 0in.
Robe, Gent's Fitted
Robe. Was £76.

Now **£65**

Furniture Bargains
1 ONLY—
4ft. 0in. SIDEBOARD
Slightly marked. £22.
Now **£12**
KITCHEN STOOLS
All colours **30/-**
**2-SEATER LEBUS
SUITE** in green .. **£59**

Ladies' Dept.

F.F. BUTTON-UP CARDIGAN
(each) **29/11**
(All sizes)
W.M. and O.S. Cotton
Knit
LUMBER JACKETS
(each) **15/-**

Shop in comfort at Macclesfield's Walk Round Store
Where service and satisfaction is guaranteed
18-20-22 CHESTERGATE, MACCLESFIELD
TELEPHONE MACCLESFIELD 2619

What could be purchased at Holland and Barwoods in Chestergate in 1962.

70

A Gill of Milk at St George's

"School, for most children of my vintage, began when they were four years of age, or as soon as practicable after one's fourth birthday. As far as I know, there was no such thing as pre-school classes or kindergartens, it was straight to school.

Boys will be boys – a 1933 group at St George's

"I was born and brought up in Saville Street, Macclesfield, and the first school I attended was St George's School, although St Peter's School on Windmill Street was much nearer. I suspect that I was sent to St George's School because my older brothers may have attended there, and certainly my elder sister was still at school when I first attended, and I have vague recollections of her taking me to school at various times. One thing was certain, you got plenty of exercise going to and from school, for I went down Saville Street, then down Windmill Street, crossed

71

over Mill Lane at Bowers' Corner, and then the climb up Chapel Street until you reached the school. Of course it was no better on the return journey, but at least you were heading home.

"St George's School was located on High Street, at the corner of Chapel Street. I recall it as a large, box-like two storey building, surrounded by a high brick wall with flat coping stones on the top. Entrance to the school was via two huge wrought iron gates, which seemed to be painted dark green. The high brick wall surrounded the playground which was divided into two by a smaller wall. The yard farthest away from Chapel Street was for the babies class (first year children) and the girls; the playground which included the iron gates was for the boys. There was a much larger playground on the other side of Chapel Street, in the shape of a large square, this was surrounded by a wall, about four or five feet in height and edged with trees. The surface of the playground was solid tarmac. This area had in fact been a graveyard for St George's Church and there were still a few grave stones around the edge of the playground.

"Considering I was at that school from the age of four until I was eleven, not a lot of memories remain. Yet I can recall that the entrance to the babies class, as it was called, was up a ramp at the back of the school, and two of the teachers names that come to mind are a Miss Carnforth and a Mr Pearson.

"The school caretakers were a Mr and Mrs Mitchell, and their house was next to the school on the southern side of the building, which meant that their back door came into the school yard and I remember them as kindly folk. One of the rules of the day was that each child should have a bottle of milk – usually a gill, eighth of a pint – I hated milk, particularly in winter, when the milk could be so cold there would be ice in it. I recall the Mitchells taking on the task of turning the cold milk into hot cocoa, for the young children. Whether this was part of their official duties or not, I have no idea, but it was greatly appreciated. The milk bottles in those days came with cardboard tops. There were flat circular pieces of card inside the top of each bottle. The milk bottle top had a circular impression stamped in the middle, the idea was that you punched this in to make a way for your straw, a good idea, but a number of children ended up wearing most of their milk allowance if there was a batch of faulty tops.

"Much is made of recycling these days, but we were doing such things in those days, not so much to keep the environment tidy, but out of sheer necessity. The milk bottle tops were saved, washed and allowed to dry and then were used for raffia work. We were taught how to layer the raffia around the cardboard tops and then link them together to make such things as table mats and teapot stands.

"The headmaster of the school was Mr Binks, who was know to the children as 'Billy Binks', though he was always addressed as Mr Binks. There was also another male teacher at the school, Mr Dale, again known to the children as 'Sammy Dale'. Mr Dale went on to become the headmaster of St George's following Mr Bink's untimely death. Both men must have been long suffering and patient men, for the headmaster's office was a cubby hole at the top of the stairs, about the size of two telephone boxes, for if the office seemed small to a child, what impression must this have made on the adults?

"Another stalwart of the staff was Miss Pixton, and to this day I have no idea of her Christian name. She was regarded by the children as something of a dragon at times, but her attitude to the children was always fair. Miss Pixton had the responsibility of organising the Rose Queen Pageant. I've no idea what the Rose Queens did, or how they were selected, or why, but I can recall being involved in at least one of these productions. I was one of a group of Toy Soldiers who had to march in a wooden fashion, with stiff arm and leg movements, it would have been enough to make any self-respecting RSM cry! We were drilled for hours, or so it seemed, by Miss Pixton, marching backwards and forwards across that tar-macadam playground. On the day, which was always a Saturday, we assembled at school already dressed in our 'uniform' ready to take part in the procession around the streets surrounding the school. Under the trees at the far end of the playground, a wooden stage had been erected, complete with throne, where the Rose Queen would be crowned once we had finished the parade. The Toy Soldiers marched, other characters walked, some of the girls danced, and the Rose Queen rode in style in a small car at the back of the procession. All went well for a while, with householders turning out to watch us go by, then somewhere around Pitt Street the car broke down and all the Toy Soldiers were invited to come and help push the car back to the school. So much for all the training. I seem to recall that the Rose Queen was always accompanied by a Town Crier, who was dressed in a blue and white silk top, blue pantaloons, with white socks and buckle shoes; he carried a cushion on which lay a crown for the Rose Queen. The Town Crier was always older than the rest of us, and on this occasion I believe he was a Grammar School boy by the name of Peter Robinson. Many years later Peter shot to operatic fame after winning a singing scholarship to Milan, and he then became known as Forbes Robinson.

"My favourite teacher was Miss Warren, again I don't know her Christian name. She was always Miss Warren, even when I met her again, years after leaving school. I found out much later that Miss Warren was one of the family of Warren Bottlers of Catherine Street. I seem to recall that Miss Warren was one of the teachers who taught me handwriting, as opposed to printing. We used steel-nibbed pens with plain wooden handles, with ink pots at the back of the desks, and woe betide anyone who got ink spots on their work. At least one of the children in the class would be appointed ink monitor, and it was their responsibility to see that the ink pots were washed out and filled with fresh ink each week. I think I liked Miss Warren because she was the only person I knew at that time who had been to Australia. She could even help me understand some of the things my brother Laurence had written from Australia. Not that he wrote that often, but he had a terrible script, and even my parents had great difficulty in deciding what he had written, so Miss Warren was a great help even outside her teaching role.

"I can recall that the newly-elected Mayor of the Borough used to visit us, and this seemed to result in us getting a half day off. I seem to recall one gentleman saying that one day, someone in that class could well become the Mayor of Macclesfield. I wonder if anyone made it, or was that a message he gave in each school?

"One of the events I do recall was the celebration at school of the Coronation of King George the Sixth. Again, we had a visit from the Mayor, who presented each child with a boxed silk handkerchief depicting King George and Queen Elizabeth, to mark the occasion, and I had mine for many years. I believe these were made of Macclesfield silk and may have been produced locally. I remember that we had some kind of celebration party at school, although I can't remember what happened. I do recall that we had strict instructions to arrive at school that day carrying a teaspoon and a mug. I also recall we ended the day with a mugful of Eddie Granelli's ice cream, provided by the teachers.

"St George's School did leave its mark on me physically, as one day I was running around the playground with others, playing some kind of childish games, when I tripped over the roots of one of the trees and went flying head first and bashed my teeth on one of the remaining gravestones. I was taken home and I recall sitting on the back lawn in a deck chair, eating large quantities of ice cream to help cool things down. The pain went away after a couple of days, but I was left with a dent in my two front teeth and they remained at that peculiar angle until they were removed many years later.

"The gravestones didn't last long after that ... it was nothing to do with my accident, rather the advent of World War II. Brick and concrete air raid shelters were built in the school playground, and it wasn't long before we were having class drills for donning our gas masks and also emergency evacuations to the shelters. Fortunately neither of these procedures were put to the test under fighting conditions.

Central School for Boys

"Around the age of eleven, I was fortunate enough to pass the entrance examination to the Central School for Boys. The boys' classes were located on the upper floor of the building, and the girls attended school on the ground floor and never the twain could meet. At that time a school uniform was required, but I think this eventually fell by the wayside, because of the difficulty of getting enough clothing coupons to provide uniforms.

The school consisted just of the main building, with a domestic science section for the girls and woodwork area for the boys in a separate single storey construction. As I recall, all the boys' teachers were male, and in the beginning the masters wore black gowns, and the headmaster, Mr A Houseman, wore a black gown and mortar board, and the boys lined up in classes in the yard before being admitted for morning assembly.

"The classes, as I remember them, were arranged as follows:

"The first classroom on the left-hand side, at the top of the stairs, at the Byron Street end was the Maths room, and home of Form One. This was presided over by Mr Eb Kirk, the Maths master, and he had the knack of getting the class's attention in no uncertain terms. Should the class start to get a little unruly, several things happened at once, all in the space of about five seconds. Mr Kirk would rise behind his desk, fix the offender with a baneful eye, slam down the lid of his desk with tremendous force, and roar at the top of his voice: "BOY! Do you want a stripe?" Needless to say, he got our attention immediately. I should explain that a stripe was a kind of demerit point and not physical violence. But he was a good bloke, and it must have been a struggle to implant the theory of Maths and Algebra into our young minds.

"Next door was Harry Trickett, the language teacher: one year's intake would be taught French, the next year the new intake would learn Spanish, and much to my disgust I dropped for a Spanish year. He too was a good teacher but we did try to inveigle him into telling us tales of his travels in Spain.

"The middle classroom was the domain of Mr Jackson, the Geography teacher. Mr Jackson was always known by his nickname of Ticker Jackson, the only reason for this I could conclude was perhaps he always wore a pocket watch and never a wrist watch. Mr Jackson also provided the piano music for morning assembly and he struggled manfully to keep us in tune and on time, in morning prayers.

"Mr Blackford, or Bill Blackford, had the next classroom, where he tried to teach us the finer points of English; he too was a kindly man.

"The last classroom on that side of the building was the

home of the history teacher, Mr Rhodes ... I won't record his nickname, but I never knew how he came by such a name. However he drummed into us the importance of history, and something must have sunk into our skulls. A few steps down the corridor on that side of the building was the Headmaster's Study, and if you saw any boy waiting outside there was a good chance that he would be on the carpet for some misdemeanour or other.

Macclesfield Cricket Club team at the end of the Second World War.

"This left two classes on the first floor; just about opposite to the History Room was the Art Room, presided over by Daddy Brocklehurst. I seem to recall that he had a good aim with a piece of chalk, a sure-fire way of getting your attention should your mind wander.

"At the other end of the assembly hall was the Science Room, this was under the direction of Mr Francis, and amid the Bunsen burners we began to have a small understanding of what Science was all about.

"There was one other teacher left, and that was Johnny Coups. He taught woodwork to all the boys and we came to appreciate the qualities of wood and the importance of having sharp chisels and saws.

"I don't know what the drill is these days for classes, but we used to go from room to room, depending on the subject being taught at that hour of the day. Someone used to teach us physical education, in the school yard, or if we were lucky on the playing field, but this was mainly of the arm stretch or jumping up and down variety, and yet the highlight of the sports year was the Cross Country run, yet I can't recall ever having any training in such matters.

"On the appropriate day, all the boys would be in sports gear and in the yard waiting for the off. When the race was started, we ran down Byron Street and over Cross Street – with no lollipop ladies to direct the traffic. I don't know how the other boys fared, but at this stage I had run out of puff, to put it politely. Then it was off up Byrons Lane, turn right into Bullocks Lane and head for the canal. Turn right onto the canal, and then along the towpath as far as the Bone Works. Here we turned right and travelled over Turf Moss until we got to Moss Lane. Then it was around the outside of the football ground and on to London Road. At the bottom of London Road, at the junction of South Street, it was up the rough ginnel to take us out near White's Dyehouse and then along High Street and back to the school. There was a rumour circulating the classroom when I got back, near the end but not the last, to the effect that I had fallen into the canal. I am pleased to record that such a thing did not happen to me.

"From time to time we had visiting speakers to the school and I can recall two of them for totally different reasons. One was an American Major, who was stationed at Tytherington Hall. In honour of his visit, Mr Jackson started to teach us the American National Anthem, The Star Spangled Banner. He did quite well, and then in came the expert in the shape of Mr J L Riley of J L Riley Choir fame. From the word go he attacked the piano with great gusto, and as it creaked and groaned, showers of dust could be seen falling from the back of the instrument. He must have enthused us, for on the day the American Major was most impressed that we know all the verses of his National Anthem, by heart. He had to spoil it though by asking if we know all the verses of our National Anthem, by heart.

Just before the outbreak of the Second World War ... how times have changed!

"The other speaker I remember was a Chinese missionary. One thing he said has stuck in my mind ever since. He drew Chinese characters on the board and drew illustrations alongside. There was a sun in the sky, shining over a roof, and underneath the roof was a pig. The literal translation of the Chinese characters read: "All under heaven one family".

"On one occasion an appeal was made in morning assembly for volunteers to go out potato picking. As most of the able bodied men were then in the forces or various reserved occupations, the farmers desperately needed help to raise the potato crop and some of the boys from the Central School went to help.

"Another job which involved input from the Central School Boys was the planting of pine trees in the Macclesfield Forest, around Trentabank, I think. If memory serves me correctly, one of the boys from my class was singled out for special mention for his dedication in planting trees, he was Philip Powell and Philip had a hand in planting more of the trees than anyone else. The last time I saw Philip, he was a manager for the MEPS at the John Street Branch.

"Since then, the boys have become scattered all over the world. I wonder where they are now?"

Happy days: Christ Church school playground, 1947

14

Thick Orange Juice and Cod Liver Oil

Mrs Susan Rumsay (née Brocklehurst) now lives in Marsh Green, Biddulph, but was born and bred in Macclesfield and has many delightful memories of her years here. In fact (and I know she won't mind me telling you) she was born on the 29th of December 1944, at number 13 Rowan Way, Hurdsfield. Her father was born in Duke Street but spent most of his early life at 43 Arbourhay Street, and her mother, born in Hatton Street, later moved to Monsall Drive.

The following is just a part of her recollections of those early Hurdsfield childhood days and a journey into town. The remainder will, I hope, he incorporated in another volume of Macclesfield Memories at a later date.

"When I was born, my Dad was 'away'. He didn't go into the army, he was doing lead burning 'making bombs' they used to tell me. He went to Scotland and Wrexham. I know Nurse Robinson 'brought' me and there was talk of 'Doodle Bugs and Blind Buzzers' and I thought of insects flying around the room. I have never liked big moths or flying beetles in the room – it was many years before I realized that they were the weapons of war.

"My memories of Rowan Way are lovely. On the corner of Queens Avenue was Mr & Mrs Walker. He was my uncle's brother; next Parkers, then Miss King's. Hamlets – he was a Policeman and for some reason used to organise trips on a 'Charra' to pantomimes etc. Next was Maurice and Doris

Newton – he had a shoe shop on Church Wallgate with his father; Charlie and Joan Bennison – he had a cobblers; next door to us were the Hallams. Mr & Mrs and an old lady; I think it was Mrs Hallam's mother or grandmother – I just remember she was very, very old, their daughter Mary and son-in-law Selwin and Janet, a little girl with bright red curly hair; we shared an entry, then us, then Mr & Mrs Cuncliff and Arthur; next door I can't recall but later came the Albinsons, then a bungalow in the corner, Burgesses – Jean and Paula – and later Gillian, then Miss Embleton and Berty – Mr & Mrs Frelan, the Weavers – he was a Policeman, Mrs Leigh and Reggie, Uptons, Campeys, Cotterills and Fred Cotterill was the school inspector. For late-coming or more serious offences he would visit parents; next were the Ormes and next Mr & Mrs Picker. There were fields and my Auntie Alice and Uncle Frank's house next, then Sands, then Mr Hooley and Flora, his daughter, who we paid rent to at first and on the other corner I think, Harrisons. I would watch the farmer making hay in the field – he also brought the milk round with a horse and cart. I think his name was Mr Nixon.

"Eventually, Brock Whistons built some houses across there for the workers from the factory in Hurdsfield Road, many of the people in Rowan Way worked at 'Brocks'.

"As I said, my Auntie Alice and Uncle Frank lived across from us and my Auntie Muriel and Uncle Stan lived up Spinney Mead with my cousins Joan and Peter. Peter was older than us, Joan about 18 months older than me. I was taken up there to play with them, but I remember going across to Auntie Alice's to 'help her'. I washed the fruit for baking – eating most of the raisins, standing on a stool I did this for hours and sat in her garden in the afternoons, I think probably more towards the end of 1946 which was when we were having another baby – Nurse Fairclough would be bringing this baby as Nurse Robinson was not around any more. I think she was moved to another area or retired but Nurse Fairclough lived on Nicholson Avenue and whenever I saw her going out with her black bag I thought she was taking another baby in there for some lucky people!

82

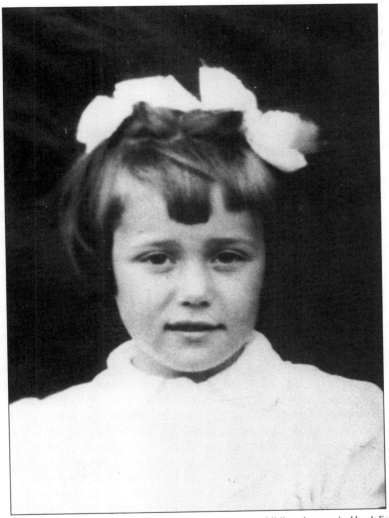

Susan Rumsay, nee Brocklehurst, pictured during her childhood years in Hurdsfield.

"My mum had had an accident in the kitchen just before my brother was born. She used to hang clothes on a little line in the kitchen in winter and climbing up on something to do this had slipped and put her foot in the boiler – it was badly scalded and I remember bandages – I hated bandages – so I can remember having to be persuaded to go in to see my new brother, because my mum still had the bandages on her foot but they got me in and I looked into a Moses Basket and saw a lovely baby but the best thing was the smell of him. I loved baby powder and things and white shawls, and he always had bootees that fell off.

"Winters were always very cold and this one was no exception. There always seemed to be lots of snow.

"My dad had started a business as a plumber in a back room at my Uncle Billy's barbers shop in Old Park Lane. He used to push his tools round on a hand cart and he went to work on a big green bicycle with very high handlebars, my mother called it 'The Stag'. I used to wait sometimes walking down Rowan Way to see him come round the corner and then it was tea time.

"We didn't have to shop very much for food as an order was taken in to Ernie Hulmes which was next to my Uncle's barbers shop and it would arrive in a cardboard box – unpacking it was always exciting, sometimes there were Cadbury's chocolate biscuits, three-cornered ones. We had two little shops close by on each corner of Lowerfield Road: Mrs Bradley's and Miss Leah's. We went to Miss Leah's for bread and fruit and veg or whatever was available, there were always buckets with celery in, I hated the smell of those and have never eaten the stuff. Sometimes it was rhubarb in the buckets, I liked that. Other times we would walk up to Hurdsfield Co-op. We passed the Flowerpot on the corner of Mason's Lane and there was a big parrot in a cage in a small window, I always stopped to look at that. We would call at Billy Buxton's butchers shop – his wife, Edna, was a dressmaker in the back of the shop where they lived – she made clothes for my mother and me, mine were usually made from something of my mothers. Opposite was Hurdsfield Church. I always thought how big it was; on up to the Co-op. The man made a bag out of blue paper and put some white powder into it for me, they called it Kali. I don't know what it was but it was a bit fizzy. Sometimes I ate it with liquorice sticks or fingers! We went down to the bottom of Hurdsfield Road on Friday afternoons 'to pay the papers' at Mr

Spearing's and called at Miss Yates little wool shop on the corner of Steeple Street. She sold wool, cotton, silks etc, elastic and various other items we always needed. Mr Brown's was on the corner of Smythe Street – he had toys and sweets and it was more fun looking in there. We went to Nixons coal yard to pay for and order coal and my mother would tell him not to send too much slack or various other types of requests would be made. The office was a green shed with a heater in that smelt awful; I suppose it was paraffin or something. We would walk back along by the Bollin and the water was always different colours – my mum said it was dye from the mills. We'd pass the Barracks Mill and see this stuff gushing out into the river, on past the gas works and up Nicholson Avenue home.

"I recall one day when we went to the Co-op on Sunderland Street for some item of linen. I thought that was fine shop with lots of wood and glass, a large stair case with brass banisters leading to the ladies and children's clothes section. My mum worked in the Co-op Bank during the war so she would know the ladies in there and they would like to see us; we were late coming home and it was going dark. The gas lamps were lit and it began to rain, we ran along and past the cattle pens under the bridge to Commercial Road and it rained more, we reached the public toilets on Commercial Road and I was lifted into the pram with my brother, John, who was just a baby still. The rain made a puddle on the apron and I was playing with the water and pulling it in my mouth. I was told not to do this, the water had germs in. We ran up Garden Street which was cobblestones then and there was water everywhere. There was always a good smell of baking down on Commercial Road at a small bakery next to Pearn's Chemists, so we always felt hungry when we got home.

"Some days we would go up to my Grandma's on Monsall Drive – we would go along Higher Fence Road and Swans Pool so I took some bread for the ducks and swans; that was great fun, standing by the railings throwing bread in. At the back of the pool was a big house, the people would sometimes pass in big cars. They were very posh people with smart clothes. My Grandpa had arthritis and I don't remember a time when he worked at Hovis although he had done so; he had a lovely garden with fir trees at the bottom. I loved the smell of these trees and looking over the wall at the bottom. Sometimes there were cows in there.

"My mum was one of five children: Auntie Muriel, Uncle Frank, next my mother Kathleen, then Uncle Stanley and the youngest – Uncle Douglas. The two youngest boys 'went missing' in the war and never came home. There was always a sad feeling when they talked about them, even though I was so young I can remember that feeling and the photographs of them in their RAF uniforms.

Bowling was a popular pastime in Macclesfield parks during the twenties, thirties and forties ... In fact it wained but little in the 50s and today Macc can claim some top class players.

"When my dad was at home on Sundays he would take me down to the Victoria Park. He would sit by the bowling green and I would play around. Once I stood on the grass and I was shouted at. I never walked on a bowling green again. We would go through the gates into Daybrook Street. The park keeper's house was on the left-hand side going out and the swings were there. We would go down into Arbourhay Street and visit my

Grandparents at number 43. They had adopted a girl called Mary and she would be there. They would be cooking dinner, meat in a large black fireside oven and always a rice pudding in there. This was such a quiet house, my Grandparents and Auntie Mary were deaf and dumb, or 'stone deaf' as it was called in those days.

"They spoke to each other in sign language and I never got the hang of that! I suppose this is why my Grandad was a big gentle person to me – he's pick my brother up with his big hands and smile and obviously made no sound. He took me to his ducks and hens, they were behind Brock Whiston's mill alongside Landsdown Street. I expect he rented the land from the mill owners. He was very proud of his ducks. Originally the idea was to have them for lunch at Christmas and special occasions, but they used to follow him around and he became too fond of them so they remained. Grandad was a boilerman at BWA and he collapsed at work and died.

"I don't know when it was I started Sunday School. I always seemed to go to Sunday School at Fence Street Chapel. Miss Lean, I think, would take us down, several of us – I was in Miss Boothby's class. It was at the back of the actual chapel. We sat on little wooden chairs – it was dusty in there and hot in summer. There was a big piano and Miss Boothby played and sang hymns like: 'Jesus wants me for a Sunbeam'. I saw the dust shining in the sun streaming in through the many windows – yes, that must be a sunbeam! I asked my mum and she said yes – I could not imagine how to become one of those!

"Chapel was good – there were concerts, plays by the older members, field treats, sales of work at Christmas and The Sermons. Concerts actually took place in the Chapel – the stage where the choir sat would be cleared and we would do the concerts there or just in front of the stage on a raised area. I remember one time each child was given a Nursery Rhyme to enact – suitable to their name if possible. I was given Mary, Mary, Quite Contrary – as my name is Susan Mary. I remember Miss Boothby saying that was very suitable for me! Oh dear, I can remember being quité contrary in Miss Boothby's class.

Holy Trinity Sunday School banner is proudly held aloft in the annual parade on Hurdsfield Road in 1960 by Mr Fred Morton (left) and Mr Jack Cobham.

"The plays we had to watch with our parents they made a proper stage with curtains etc, very professional they were. It was a bit boring for very little children but we had to 'sit good'. I stayed awake but my brother always fell asleep.

"The Field Treats were very exciting. Occasionally we went on a train but I can't recall where to. We played games and had picnics and ice cream – they took all kinds of things along.

"The Sale of Work was magic, but then it was near Christmas. There were stalls selling sheets, table cloths etc. My mum bought 'Thrift' tickets for months, saved them up and bought pillow cases, towels, sheets etc. There was a bran tub – strange things were picked out from the bottom of the bran or sawdust. I once had a butterfly made from silver with holes in. It was a tree decoration. It has now vanished, but lasted for many years.

"Father Christmas I know must have been there and always someone very important to 'open' the Sale. One time it was someone called John Mills. He had belonged to the Chapel years ago and my dad came along to see him – he had been a friend of his. I thought this was John Mills and actor and got very confused when told that it was just the same name.

88

It is 1960 and the venue is Daybrook Street before the annual sermons parade. Barbara Whittaker is the rosebud queen. Also pictured are Mrs Joyce Kirkham, Elsie Weaver and Alice Axford.

"Preparing for the Sermons went on for weeks. We learned what hymns we would sing and had a little booklet or paper printed. Two men carried an organ round and we stopped to sing at various points along the route. We all had new clothes – if it was likely to be hot a dress and cardigan, if cool a hat and coat – new shoes, even socks and I always had new ribbons for my hair. We carried flowers. In the afternoon there was a service in Chapel and our flowers were placed round the front and even in the doorways. Some people would sing solos and there was usually an important singer or a special preacher and it was all very grand. I am certain that once, in the early days, we had Peter Robinson, later to become the famous Forbes Robinson. My mother was always a keen fan of his, running out into the garden to 'jump up and down' calling to Mrs Albinson – next door but one – who came out and did the same, when he won some singing competition – we were listening to it on the radio. We would also go back in the evening to continue the sermons with yet another service in Chapel – every pew and form and chair that could be used was used, the place was packed.

"We had a Christmas party – always potted meat sandwiches and lovely fresh bread, cakes, jellies, junkets, blancmanges, orange juice, tea made in an urn – lots of fun and games.

"When I was a little older I went morning and evening to Sunday School. Mr Leah and Mr Kirkham took us down. Mr Moss often lead the service in the Chapel, the little ones sitting at the front on the little wooden chairs and forms and older ones in the pews at the back.

"It didn't seem long until I was old enough to go with my cousin, Joan, and later to take my brother – on my own – I walked up Smythe Street and along Arbourhay Street because I could always smell the Sunday joints cooking in the cottages and old ladies, sat on the doorsteps in the doorways on chairs, or even at the front of the cottages, would talk to us as we passed. Opposite my Grandma's house was an old lady called Mrs Higginbotham – she never had any teeth in but she was always smiling. I was always instructed to go straight to Chapel and straight home and not to dawdle, but sometimes I was a bit late either way – imagine letting small children go along to anywhere on their own today – you can't! I even ventured into the Victoria Park to watch boys playing football on the playing field or occasionally the swings but usually they were locked up on Sundays – did we climb the gates? Surely not! Another place we may have called was the Tip on Nicholson Avenue – this was just some waste ground but we were told not to go there so it made us curious.

"Going 'Up Town' must have taken hours, when we had the big pram it was either down Commercial Road and up Hibel Road but there were so many things to look at. Along Commercial Road opposite the waste ground – where I remember the Salvation Army band playing sometimes, was a little shop called the 'Dairy'. I don't know to this day why it was so called, but it was a little old lady with thin grey hair tied back in a bun. She had a large window displaying a few goods dotted about, some of which were lollies and liquorice. I always stopped to look but didn't always get anything. Next came the Cattle Market: that was a hustle and bustle on market day –

wagons were there; cows, pigs, sheep being pushed into pens by a man we always called 'Corporation Ken' who had brown leather leggings, boots, corduroy trousers and an old mac with a leather belt round the waist. Later, as I recall, he had wellingtons and string around his waist, but I'm sure it was always the same mac. He also helped out clearing up after the market and brushing streets in these areas. Under the bridge at the bottom of Buxton Road there were more pens on the left. In a corner there was a wooden shed or two where lots of farmers with their walking sticks would be congregating. Each section of the pens had certain animals – my favourite of course were the calves.

"Across to the Waters there was a cafe on the corner – Arrowsmiths. Their daughter, Barbara, later came to our school. Waters Green was all cobblestones, pubs and a few market stalls, although the main market was in front of the old Church.

"Up Church Wallgate – that was a push with the pram, especially on hot days – Newtons shoe shop and bike shop then across to the food office – we got thick orange juice and cod liver oil in flat bottles. Janet Foot next door had some lovely sticky stuff in a carton but we could never have that. Why, I don't know; I expect it was because we got big brown jars of cod liver oil and malt from Hadfields, that was lovely. I later discovered that Janet's cartons contained Virol. My mother used to put the orange juice in a Bakelite cup – orange and speckled – I still have that cup and can remember warm water went into the orange from the kettle and always the cod liver oil went in and floated on the top. The orange was lovely but the cod liver oil ruined it – my mum put it in without me seeing and pretended it was just orange juice, but I could always see it floating on the top.

"We would go to Pott & Thomsons for the ground coffee, made up in paper bags. My dad always made coffee with milk and coffee grounds, boiling up on the stove. He put it in a blue jug with a lid – really a coffee pot – it smelt lovely and so did the shop where we bought the coffee. I would stand at the window and look at the big red coffee machine, watching the beans being tipped in at the top and all the coffee grounds coming out of a shoot at the other end.

Staff of Seymour Meads (in the late fifties) in the Market Place: Kath Whiston (left), Louis Baker, Doris ?, Gertie Unwin, Roy Spragg (manager), David Hodkinson, John Roberts, Kath Cotterill (who kindly supplied the picture).

"There was a little jeweller's shop next door and I had to look in there for ages, very interesting; a furniture shop, the Army and Navy, Bradleys (not very interesting) then Whitings toys and 'Muriel', a dress shop. I liked standing looking here as well. We began to have our meat delivered from Joe Forrest's so we'd go to give the order or pay the bill. We never went further down Chestergate very often and I was glad because I did not like the things hanging outside Harry Potts little shop – dead birds and rabbits, horrible! My mum would buy stockings and underwear from Maisie Benson's. My mum thought she was a bit dear but my dad did work for them so we had to go there. Cartledge's cake shop had all the cakes in the window, although mum baked her own I could sometimes persuade her to buy some. There was a sweet shop on the corner of Derby Street and the Toc H. What was this? I thought for years that they made light bulbs because the saying "dim as a Toc H light bulb" must have been used when I was very young. How else would I get this idea? My mother's hairdresser had a little shop in Church Street West (Mrs Birchenough). There was a big wooden gate at the side behind which Mr Trotter kept things.

"I would always look in at the Avery Scales. I don't know what the attraction was, but maybe it was to do with my fascination for little shops. I thought I'd have one when I grew up. We'd see if my dad's handcart was outside the shop and if it was we would call on him. It was always great fun playing around at 43 Stanley Street and my mother would take me through to the toilet and then carry on with the shopping.

"In Castle Street was a cafe, the ladies in there were wearing dresses and hats that appeared in Muriel's window, I thought. I used to watch them; I think we went in very occasionally if my mother saw someone she knew. The lady who owned the cafe was very smart with wavy hair. She had a strange way of talking and she sounded a bit like someone on the wireless to me!

"Down on to Mill Street to Woolworths, I hated that because the counters were high and I couldn't see anything. On down Mill Street to Old Park Lane to call in on Uncle Billy Walkers barbers shop, 31 Old Park Lane, I think. His shop was interesting: lots of cupboards with glass sliding doors, tobacco, Swan Vestas, cigarettes, Woodbines, Players, Craven A with a little black cat on the packet, Brylcream, scented water – would this be cologne or after-shave? It went on people's faces after the shave. Uncle Billy always said I could help in the shop one day when I was big enough, and I did.

"Next, into Ernie Hulmes, probably to give the order, and the cheese. Oh! My mother had problems with the cheese, she told him it was like soap.

"We called in Nadin's for fish. Usually I liked plaice, but we sometimes had cod or 'finney haddock', yellow and strong tasting – I didn't like that.

"We walked home along Sunderland Street, sometimes calling in the Co-op. My mother called all Co-ops 'The Stores', and sometimes she just talked to the ladies and showed us off. If my dad needed hats or braces or anything to wear, we had to get it from him from the Co-op Men's Wear; they were very helpful and knew what size to give us. Once we bought a very fine Trilby – I think it must have been his birthday. The whole shop seemed to be disrupted, hats were everywhere, you had to choose well, it had to last forever!"

Chris Paling's pantomimes were much looked forward to in Macclesfield during the 1940s and '50s. In 1951 the Majestic Cinema was host to 'Snow White' and here is the cast. Back row, left to right, standing: Keith Westbrook, Grant Turner, Leslie Biggar, Norman Bingham, Bill Davidson, Joan Milkler, Chris Paling, Norman Clarke, John Worsley, Jack Burgess; middle row: Graham Carrol, Rhona Walton, Geoff Morris, Jean Patterson, Jimmy Chatterton, Hilary Martin; front: Linda Moss, Janice Hosker, Christine Bailey. Picture: J Burgess.

Opposite: Popular in the pantos at the Majestic were the Norjack Acrobats, pictured, comprising Jack Burgess, who supplied this picture, Norman Bingham and Linda Moss. They were participating in Babes in the Wood at the Majestic when this photo was taken. During 1951 they competed in a talent contest at Buxton and were awarded first prize, forcing into second place a talented young bass singer from Macclesfield. His name was Peter Forbes Robinson who later that year won the coveted Great Caruso contest promoted by film star Mario Lanza. As Forbes Robinson, he trained at La Scala, Milan, and achieved world-wide fame with the Covent Garden Opera Company. I knew Forbes very well and he always had a soft spot for his home town, returning whenever he was able to. Unfortunately he passed away some years ago.

94

15

Watching Ack-Ack from my Bedroom Window

Maurice Winnell joined the Home Guard as soon as he was able, at the age of 17. Before that he had been used by the Civil Defence Volunteers as a messenger. Today he can still relate where all the local defence sites were situated and has a comprehensive collection of photos of the remaining ones. I have had the interesting pleasure of being taken to some of these by Maurice, who I class as an expert on Macclesfield's War Years. The following is just part of his recollections:

"Civilian gas-masks were issued in 1938 at the time of the Munich crisis, I remember queuing at St John's school to be issued with one, at the same time hoping that no agreement was reached nationally to prevent me getting one. At the beginning of the war it was necessary to carry the gas mask in order to gain admittance to the cinema etc.

"People got used to the blackout, white lines were painted around trees and lamp-posts and people carried small torches, the amount of light emitted was cut down by a piece of slotted cardboard or tissue paper inserted under the glass. The same thing was done to bicycle lamps.

"As a lad of 15 I worked at Hollingdrake's Garage, Prestbury, and I fitted V Hartley headlamp masks to the headlights of cars. They were a hooded device and were very effective. Bumpers and a strip along the running boards were painted white. Petrol went on ration, five gallons a month unless the driver qualified for extra through war work or employment as a doctor etc. Just before rationing commenced people were rushing to the garage with every variety of container and filling up to try to get a reserve in hand. I found that very amusing.

"Quite a few people laid their cars up for the duration, they put the car up on bricks etc and took the wheels off. They took the spark plugs out and squirted oil into the cylinders turning the engine over by hand to spread the oil onto the cylinder walls, and the cars came through the war in good condition.

"When the air-raids on Manchester got into their stride (1940-41) I mended many punctures in car tyres caused by anti-aircraft shrapnel picked up in the streets of the Manchester area by Prestbury residents who worked there. The thin slivers of shrapnel penetrated the tyres as easily as any nail.

"There were a number of searchlights in the vicinity of Macclesfield and while they were taking part in their exercises, sweeping the sky, it made the streets markedly lighter by the reflected light from the clouds. We found it a boon when walking about the town.

"From my bedroom window I could see the Ack Ack shells bursting over the Stockport and Manchester area, also the searchlights trying to pick out the German aircraft, occasionally I would see a Chandelier flare descending in the distance. We got used to the German aircraft droning overhead on their way to Manchester, the only danger was if one decided to jettison his bomb load.

"Air-raid shelters were built in Macclesfield at the beginning of the war, the first ones that I remember were trenches dug in the South Park close to the football pitches. They were roofed over with planks and sandbags. Later brick-built shelters were erected all round Macclesfield and the only ones I know that still exist are two at the bottom of Old Park Lane near to the library buildings (to be removed, I understand).

"The first air-raid warning that sounded one night shortly after the war began caused a bit of a panic in my area of Barton Street and Vincent Street. Some people rushed out of their houses to go to the shelters, leaving doors open and lights on. Later on when we all became accustomed to the siren, knowing that the enemy aircraft would pass over on their way to Manchester, people mostly just turned over in bed and slept on (apart from those who had to turn out for duty with the A.R.P. etc).

Two photographs showing the Co-op windows in Park Green during the Second World War. It was an appeal for war-workers to make silk parachutes and also rubber lifeboats.

There were many war industries in Macclesfield and there was much work to be done for those who did not go off to fight.

"When the raids on Manchester were at their height the messenger boys of the A.R.P. were expected to turn out every time (12 midnight, 1 a.m., 2 a.m. were quite normal), I was asleep on my feet during the day at work at Hollingdrake's Garage, Prestbury. So a rota system was instituted and we turned out every other time (a big improvement).

"I remember one exercise in which the whole A.R.P. took part. It took place at the derelict Victorian house in the middle of West Park. I was playing the part of a casualty in an upstairs room with a ticket around my neck describing my injuries. After a lengthy discussion by the rescue team on the type of knots to tie etc. I was swung out of the window on a metal stretcher roped at each corner to a pulley on a beam. Needless to say the knots slipped and I dropped 14 or 15 feet to the ground, still lying flat on my back on the stretcher. They tell me that I bounced up in the air off the ground but the pillows placed under my head saved me from any injury. The exercise was called off in the ensuing concern and after a checkup at the Infirmary I was sent home no worse for the affair.

It may have been wartime, but there was still time to have a party ... the year is 1940, Mr Jack Burgess of Lyme Avenue tells me, and the occasion is a children's party at the old St John's Church in Macclesfield. The Church was later closed and rebuilt at the Weston.

"When I was 17 I joined the Home Guard and took part in weekend schemes at Rainow and Wildboarclough. I had a long First World War Canadian rifle, we had Spigot Mortars, sticky bombs and other anti-tank weapons, cup dischargers to fire grenades from rifles and we were ready to take on the whole

German army. All the Home Guard of the area went to a demonstration at Styperson quarry near Adlington, and I remember that while watching a demonstration of anti-tank missiles fired at a tank painted on the quarry face one of the Home Guard dropped to the ground in front of me. He had been hit on the shin by the tail fin of one of the missiles, we hadn't much idea of safety distances in those days. We drilled at the top of Barton Street and in Athey Street School yard. Our headquarters was at one of the 12 Apostles' houses in Park Lane.

Workers at the premises of John Fred Collier, engineers, King Edward Street, during the Second World War. The shield being held was awarded in recognition of collecting the most money during the year for War Savings.

"Our Battalion manned an observation post on Windyway quarry; we could look right across the Cheshire Plain and the Manchester area. We manned it from early evening but I'm afraid to say that for us the war finished at midnight when we went to sleep, and we returned to Macclesfield at 6 or 7 o'clock next morning. I drove the party there and back in an old saloon car.

"On the home front, food was on strict rationing and one thing I remember was dried egg. It was a yellowish powder and when reconstituted I found it quite tasty.

"Troops were stationed in Macclesfield throughout the Second World War. The first I remember were stationed in the old Barracks in Crompton Road.

"At one time a famous Canadian Regiment was stationed here and later on the American troops were billeted in various locations – the Drill Hall, Church halls, mills etc. The Americans certainly livened the town up. A British restaurant was accommodated in the building next to Frost's mill in Park Green. This place was once a chapel and is now industrial premises. The restaurant was open to all citizens and the charge for a meal was a shilling (five new pence), for this was served a typical meal of sausage, mash and peas, also a pudding and a cup of tea. The Second World War was a time of great commitment and dedication.

16

Lucky Bags in the Phoney War

Roger Minshull now lives in Washington, Lincolnshire, but was born on the seventh of June, 1935, in Macclesfield. His father, Eric, had just started a tailoring business and his mother, Florence, was a shop assistant in the ladies' outfitters next door. He writes that the pavement outside numbers one and three Mill Lane and the rough ground of Broken Banks behind the shop comprised his whole world at the time Adolph Hitler was planning to add it to his empire. Roger started school one month before war broke out in 1939 at St George's up the hill and behind the shop, several streets of terraced brown brick and purple slate houses away, upon High Street. His memory tells him that most of those in Miss Barstow's babies' class were four years old. When war broke out, most expected fighting to start right away but first of all there was the Phoney War.

It is that wartime period recalled by Roger, who writes:

"If the bombing and shooting did not start in the first week in Macclesfield, other things had an immediate impact. Surrounded by Mother, Gran and two or three girls who worked in the shop, Marjorie, Gwen and the others I don't remember, I came home from school to find piles of black cloth heaped all over the place, while they cut and stitched blinds for the blackouts.

"Some people had black paper which was pinholed from the start and soon tore at the edges. Most had cotton cloth although I saw the occasional piece of velvet. At first two wooden laths were used, one at the top of the window, the other to weight it down at the bottom. Later, people were able to buy blinds on rollers and some had them fitted to light traps at the sides. Every window had to be covered and either one turned off the lights before going outside, or also had thick blackout curtains over the door. I took all this in my stride at the time but, looking back, one must give a nod of appreciation to the pre-war planning which had prepared so many things like the rationing and Civil Defence. Dowding is remembered for the air defence system we had in place by 1939 but some equally smart chap made sure that fifty million people suddenly had enough blackout material too.

It is 1944 and civil defence volunteers parade past Emmy Rawlinson's bakers shop in Park Lane. Keith Yearsley, who supplied the picture, lived at 83 South Park Road at the time.

"I don't know exactly when food rationing started. We kids became aware of that kind of thing only very slowly as the war went on. But about that time Mother and I and Neil (his young brother) in the pram went up Mill Lane, a street of small shops, to Mrs Longshaw's. There we collected a lucky bag – that is what Mother and Mrs Longshaw called it. When we got home from her sweet shop, tobacconists and lending library, I found the Lucky Bag contained smaller bags of sweets: caramels, fruit drops, humbugs, together with bars of chocolate, packets of chewing gum and other plunder from Aladdin's Cave. Mother said we would get an identical Lucky Bag from Mrs Longshaw every week, which meant for ever as far as my sense of time was then able to comprehend. What a marvellous war! A huge bag of sweets every week! Life was good, getting better, and everything was going to be okay.

An early wartime parade of civil defence volunteers going past Williamson's shop in West Bond Street. (K. Yearsley)

"We did eat sweets before the war but never in the huge quantities we consumed between 1939 and 1945. Before the war I can remember going to the paper shop at number five to buy thin bars of Cadbury's chocolate for which I paid one penny ha'penny and insisted that the lady put each in a triangular paper bag. I learned years later that she called into our shop every so often to collect the bags which Mother took off me because the cost of the bag was greater than the profit on the bar of chocolate. Apart from that I don't remember much about sweets before the war but when sweet rationing started, and particularly when extra food became hard to find, everyone made sure they got their full sweet shop ration each week. Consequently, while some could get less than they were used to, many people, including us, bought more.

"Some kids later in the war carried their sweet coupons in their pockets and bought sweets in any shop which had some in but we deposited all our coupons with Mrs Longshaw and visited her once a week for the goodies. It became a ritual. First she would eight out the quarters of caramels, barley sugars, pear drops, choc-o-limes, the ration for four. Then she added the Mars bars, Kit Kats, Crunchie bars, Maltesers and packets of Beech Nut chewing gum. Other kids in other shops, I suppose, chose Fry's Five Boys chocolate, P.K. gum, dolly mixtures, jelly babies and so on, but those were our favourites. Some of the brands have disappeared now and I would dearly like to taste Fry's Sandwich chocolate again; Peter's chocolate which said on the wrapper D. Peter: Inventor; and Cadbury's Blended which was wrapped in greaseproof paper and disappeared as the war ended. In contrast, Aero disappeared when the war started and I remember a crowd of ten-year-olds collecting in Buxton Road to take bites of the first post-war Aero. So the war started well for a four year old eating his way through the lucky bag each week, not knowing his teeth would have rotted away by 1950.

"Our gas masks were issued in pale brown, almost cubic, cardboard boxes with thin string to sling them over our shoulders. At first we had to carry our gas masks wherever we went, so we kids had to carry them to school. Very soon the string broke, the cardboard became dog-eared and a bit of variety began to develop from the early regimented scene. Some kids kept their gas mask cases until they fell apart or dissolved in the rain. Others got cheap 'rainproof' cotton covers. Some changed over to a variety of soft bags of all shapes, colours and sizes. I was given a maroon box in thicker cardboard, made to look a bit like leather, with a white canvas shoulder strap with a smart red central stripe; it soon became a scruffy grey.

"I remember admiring one boy who always had a slice of cold buttered toast wrapped in a greasy page of newspaper which he kept in his gas mask case for emergencies. Gas mask cases were not generally converted to lunch boxes until after the war but were used to carry other things. On the first day Mother put three brand new packets in my box. One contained a wound dressing, the second a burn dressing and the third a kind of gumshield. If I had been strafed and ambushed by a Jerry with a flame thrower on my way from Mill Lane to St George's, perhaps by a paratrooper lurking at the corner of Lowe Street, the two inch dressings would have been no use at all. In time the packets disintegrated then the dressings frayed into grubby grey and yellow fluff in the bottom of the box.

"The gumshield had a different ending. We were examining the contents of each other's boxes one playtime: bits of biscuit, packets of chewing gum, marbles, a mouse, dead beetles, some army cap badges, when somebody spotted my gumshield. It was made of brown translucent rubber with a hole at one end and a string to the tied to some part of the child to prevent choking if he gulped too much when a big German bomb hit the school with a loud bang. The gumshield was meant to prevent one biting one's tongue.

"What's that, Minnie?" I may as well own up to my nickname which was appropriate as I was the tiniest kid in the class.

"My gumshield." Self evident to anyone but this prat.

"What's it for then?

"So I won't bite me tongue.

"Hah! Minnie's got a dummy, Minnie's got a dummy, Minnie still sucks a dummy!" and so on. Mother had not foreseen the inevitable. On the way home the thoughtful defence against the Luftwaffe went down a grid.

"The gas masks weren't much better. They were supposed to keep us alive in the event of a gas attack. At that time plenty of people from their late thirties onwards could remember the gas attacks of the first world war and I suspect the issue of the masks was as much to keep up morale as actually to save anybody if the Germans did fly over and bomb us with gas.

"Again, in retrospect, I am impressed at how nearly fifty million people were issued with masks so quickly. Everyone got one, and as far as I can remember, we all got them the same week."

17

Some of our Sons

We still weep for sons of Macclesfield who did not return from Hitler's War. We still shed a tear for the sons of Macclesfield who did not return from the Kaiser's War. We should always shed a tear, and not just on Remembrance Day. They died for us to live and they died for us to be able to live, and enjoy, Macclesfield. Theirs was a sacrifice we can never repay.

The day war broke out, most people did not have any idea whatsoever what was in store. Gas masks were sought after not because we all expected to be overcome by some poisonous fumes but, perhaps, because we couldn't get into the pictures without them! That's what a young Maurice Winnell remembers, anyway!

And we were going to win the war in a matter of weeks. No-one could envisage it would go on as long as it did and no-one could envisage the vast loss of life and the way it would change the world forever. It was the time when Macclesfield, like so many other towns, lost its innocence.

Readers of *Macclesfield, So Well Remembered* will recall that I looked back on Macclesfield at War. Shortly after the book had been published I received an extremely interesting letter from Kevin Whittaker, the Secretary of the Macclesfield Historical Aviation Society. I have had the pleasure of knowing Kevin's father, Ken, for a goodly number of years and he has helped me in my researches for other books. Indeed, he even introduced me to a relative I did not know I had – the late Joe Mellor of Symondley Road, Sutton. Anyway, Kevin wrote to me and was kind enough to say that he had found it "very informative and interesting". However, he felt that more could have been encompassed concerning the wartime years of 1939 to 1945 with a view to giving a mention to some of Macclesfield's sons who went away to war, such as Sergeant Pilot Eric Samuel Bann, who was killed in his Hurricane fighter during the Battle of Britain. He mentioned that the Historical Aviation Society has photographs of him, with his wife, May, taken in the back garden at number 121 Bond Street.

The Society also has wartime photographs in its archives of the late Harry Lawson with his Wellington bomber crew before their fatal accident at Feltwell in 1941, when their aircraft crashed returning from a raid, and Harry was the sole survivor, though suffering injuries that remained with him for the rest of his life. The Society even has the full hospital medical report on his injuries sustained during the crash. I, and I know many others, will remember the late Alderman Harry Lawson with great affection. Harry dedicated his later years to Macclesfield, becoming a Councillor and later an Alderman of the old Borough (when Macclesfield was not part of a much larger authority but was responsible for itself). He was Chairman of the Housing Committee and dedicated himself to re-housing countless Maxonians. He was the guiding light behind the Victoria Park housing scheme and wanted to make it Macclesfield's pride and joy. He re-housed people for genuine humanitarian reasons and genuinely believed that what the Housing Committee was doing in the early 1960s was the right thing for everyone. His only motivation for this was an intense love of Macclesfield. I shed a tear when Harry died, as did many. He is now re-united with his Airforce chums in the sky, I feel sure.

Kevin Whittaker's letter continued that another son of Macclesfield wad Dennis Armitage, ex Squadron Leader with the DFC. He, too, fought as a Spitfire pilot during the Battle of Britain. He later commanded his own Squadron before being shot down in 1941 and becoming a Prisoner of War where he teamed up with Douglas Bader and, together, they wrote a play about life in a Prisoner of War camp. This play was put on stage in London in 1947 and ran for a number of weeks. Dennis and Douglas sold the play to the BBC in 1947. Dennis now lives in retirement in Hampshire though he returns to Macclesfield quite often to visit his old home, Sutton Hall.

Syd Gleave astride his S.G.S. motor bike on which he took part in two Isle of Man T.T. Races.

There was, wrote Kevin, the incident of the German bomber, shot down by fighter pilots from RAF Cranage, which crashed at Royal Cottage in 1941. The third Doodlebug or VI, which exploded on Seven Sister Lane and also the Airspeed Oxford RAF trainer that crashed at Henbury with the loss of three crew in 1943 were also recalled and he wrote: "This aircraft came to rest quite close to the church at Henbury and one of the houses opposite the church still has pieces from this aircraft appearing from time to time in the back garden. The same house also has the ghost of one of the airmen appearing from time to time. The apparition, dressed in flying clothes, has been seen by the owners on a number of occasions; it walks across the back garden. These houses were not built at the time of the crash.

Then, of course, there is Syd Cleave, who some will also remember for his motorbikes. Kevin wrote that he died test flying a Lancaster bomber from Woodford that flew into the ground at Birtles in 1944. I have heard from a number of people that Syd Gleave, whose famous motorbike was the SGS – the Syd Gleave Special – was flying the Lancaster over Macclesfield when it developed trouble and he managed to manoeuvre away from his home town and crashed at Birtles. I was once told it was fuel-pipe trouble but I do not know for certain. What I do know for sure is just what a character our Syd was.

He was a flyer of planes way before the war and he was a very keen sportsman as well. He once had a bet that he could play a round of golf in each of five different countries in one day. He started his wager by playing at Macclesfield, flew on to Wales then Ireland, the Isle of Man and Scotland. I'm not sure if I've got the right order here, but you get the idea! What a lad was Syd, the stories about him are legion ... he took part in the Isle of Man TT races on his SGS motorbike and he was adept at many other sports as well. He was a familiar sight in Macclesfield – as was his airplane that he often landed at fields off Congleton Road. Good old Syd.

Anyway, to return to Kevin's extremely informative letter: he adds that there are two points the Society would wish to make about this period during the war years. Firstly, the nearest ROC post was sited on Sutton Common close to where the TV tower now stands. In fact, this building is still in existence. As you drive up the road to the tower it is on the left, though now derelict. Secondly, on Christmas Eve, the 24th of December, 1940, a German raider unloaded its stick of bombs when it came under attack by an RAF night fighter. The bombs straddled Lower Grotto Farm at Over Peover (now renamed Crossley Farm) and killed Margaret and Edith Wrench who lived at the farm and also their nephew, Sydney Colin Wrench, a soldier who was home on leave and visiting his aunts. All three now lie together in Over Peover Methodist Church, so we feel that these souls were victims of the blitz.

Police and Fire Brigade records also show, Kevin told me, the event at Bosley on the 22nd of December, 1944, when a Dakota of the United States Air Force crashed there with the loss of six high ranking American Air Force Officers and three crew. The aircraft was returning to France from Burtonwood when it suffered engine failure and the pilot, who was the only survivor, tried to put down in Dawson's Farm, Bosley, but hit a tree on the summit of a hill close to the farm.

My thanks go to Kevin and members of the Aviation Society for this information given to me should I decide to do another book, which I have!

Finally, since I received this information, I've heard about the delayed action bombs that landed in a field near Gawsworth Road, just outside the boundary of Macclesfield. An Air Raid Warden, who I believe was Wilf Harrison, went to chase away children who were playing around them and he went with a policeman to assist. As Wilf and the PC were walking towards the children they saw the two officers and ran away. The bomb went off just in front of the policeman and warden who ended up in hospital but the children had been moved away in time by the two. Thank goodness.

Of course there were other sons, and daughters of Macclesfield who never returned. Far too many. Their memories will always remain and the Guardian Angel stands over their names at the Cenotaph in Park Green. May they rest in peace.

18

When the Young Princess Visited Us

When their Royal Highnesses the Princess Elizabeth and the Duke of Edinburgh visited Macclesfield on Monday, June the 27th, 1949, they received what the Macclesfield Times described as a wonderful and thrilling welcome from 50,000 people comprising the population of the borough and thousands of visitors who had streamed into the town by rail and road.

Never had the town been so resplendent as on this great day with the sunshine pouring down in golden radiance on the crowded streets and public squares from which there flashed and glowed countless flags, streamers and bunting. And never had the town echoed to such surging cheers as the people acclaimed the Royal couple on their tour. It was an unsurpassable welcome and the Princess and the Duke smiled happily as they waved their acknowledgments.

The royal couple arrived at Hibel Road Station at 10 o'clock in the morning and stepped onto the platform bedecked with flowers and streamers and were received by the Mayor of Macclesfield, Councillor F. Fowler and at the station exit the Duke inspected a detachment of the Seventh Cheshire Regiment. The Princess was presented with a bouquet by Shirley Hankinson representing the schoolchildren of the borough. Then the Royal pair drove to the Market Place where on a dais they heard the Town Clerk, Mr Walter Isaac, read an address of welcome. Inside they met local dignitaries and inspected a show-case of Macclesfield silk products and signed the visitors' book.

They later drove to the Hurdsfield Mills of Brocklehurst Whiston Amalgamated Ltd and toured the departments. They saw a range of products representative of the whole of Macclesfield's silk trade and chatted with operatives at their machines. It had been the special wish of the Royal couple, no doubt inspired by silk gifts sent by Macclesfield on the occasions of the royal wedding and the birth of Prince Charles, that they visit one of the mills and see something of the town's staple industry. At Hurdsfield they were presented with two dress lengths of silk and a box of silk handkerchiefs for the young Prince Charles.

It was a particularly proud moment for weaver Mrs Ruth Collier of 168 Hurdsfield Road who had been employed by BWA for 41 years and who wove the silk brocade, when she was introduced at the loom to the Princess.

9.30 A.M.

BOROUGH OF MACCLESFIELD "G"

Royal Visit

JUNE 27th, 1949

THE BEARER of this pass is a duly authorised escort, accompanying children from

St. George's Junior & Infant School to view the Royal procession.

NOTE:—It is essential that the instructions issued from the head teacher as to time to assemble, route to be taken, etc., are strictly complied with

Walter Isaac.

TOWN CLERK.

Town Clerk Walter Isaac signed this pass allowing a school teacher from St George's Junior and Infant School to view the royal procession.

Macclesfield had been honoured by Royal visitors on a number of previous occasions and the one which probably stands out most in the minds of the present generation is the visit of His Royal Highness the Duke of Gloucester, on October 2nd, 1929.

There were unprecedented scenes of enthusiasm in Macclesfield. The route of the Royal procession was thronged with thousands of cheering townspeople who gave His Royal Highness a welcome that would be long remembered by all present. After he had arrived in the town by car from Capesthorne, the Duke went to the Infirmary, where he saw the new extension and inspected the wards. From there he went to Langley, to carry out the main purpose of his visit – the opening of the new Trentabank Reservoir. At the entrance gates the then Mayor (Councillor Fred Wood) presented various members of the staff of the water undertaking to the Prince, and afterwards His Royal Highness accepted the gift of a golden key from the Mayor and unlocked the gates. With the Engineer responsible for the work (Dr Lapworth) and the Chairman of the Water Committee (Alderman J Hyde) he then turned on the valves to supply the town with water and formally declared the reservoir open.

This was not the first time the Duke of Gloucester had been to Macclesfield. While fulfilling a public engagement in Stockport in October 1925, he extended his programme to include Macclesfield – a gesture which was greatly appreciated by local residents.

Many Macclesfield people, including schoolchildren from miles around, went to Poynton in July 1946 to greet the King and Queen when they passed through the village on their way to Dunham Massey during their tour of Cheshire. The road leading into the village had been lined with flags and there was a large banner with the words 'Welcome to Poynton' to greet Their Majesties. There was a beautiful bouquet of red roses waiting for the Queen if, through some last minute alterations, the Royal car should halt in the village. It was not possible to carry out the ceremony, however, and the bouquet was placed on the local war memorial.

The 1948 visit of the Queen to Wilmslow was a memorable one for many in the district. Thousands from surrounding areas poured into the place to extend their loyal and affectionate greetings. In June, 1944, Macclesfield welcomed the Princess Royal to the town. As Commandant-in-Chief of the British Red Cross Society she inspected the Red Cross Hospital Supply Depot, Park Green. In 1895, the Duchess of Teck opened an exhibition of silk products at the School of Art, Macclesfield, and also visited various mills in the town.

The latest product in 1949.

Few people know that Queen Victoria once stayed here. In 1832, as the Princess Victoria, she passed through the town with her mother, the Duchess of Kent, and stayed at the Macclesfield Arms Hotel. She had been at Eaton Hall, near

Chester, the residence of the Duke of Westminster and was on her way to Chatsworth, the home of the Duke of Devonshire.

Throughout Sunday afternoon and night before that Royal Day in 1949, the streets along which the procession passed were crowded with people anxious to have a preview of the decorations. As the afternoon wore on the crowds increased in numbers and included hundreds from the outlying districts.

One motorist who stopped and asked for what the town was preparing paid the following compliment: "Well, the town is a credit to the people responsible for the decorations. You have certainly put on a grand show. I hope the weather remains fine and then you will have a marvellous day.

The town had more royal celebrations after the visit by the Princess and her husband: the Coronation took place in 1953 and here Waterloo Street is pictured dressed for the occasion with flags and bunting. Left to right are Mrs Hawkins with grandson Robert Whittaker, a postman, Myrtle Butterworth (nee Hawkins) and daughter Pam, Mr and Mrs Selman, Mrs Sharpley, name unknown, Mr Sharpley, Mrs Smith from the corner shop and child (name unknown).

Most of the sightseers had returned the day before from their annual holidays. Bronzed and attired in their summer dress, they looked a happy crowd. They stood and watched workmen putting up finishing touches to the floral decorations. The realistic flower garden in front of the dais in the Market Place and the window boxes on the Town Hall came in for much praise. One admirer stated "This just shows how a dull and grimy building can be brightened with a few flowers. Let us hope they keep the window boxes in permanently." (The window boxes were to remain a permanent feature of the Town Hall.)

Crowds stood round the doorway of the Town Hall admiring the flowers which lined the staircase and the view was expressed that the building should be thrown open to the public after the Royal couple had left. Unfortunately, the flowers inside the Town Hall, which were loaned by Salford Parks Department, had to be returned during that afternoon. There was a constant stream of visitors to Hibel Road Station where they watched the Parks Department employees erecting the banks of flowers.

The latest Bush 'de Luxe' console costing 15 guineas in 1949.

News that two of the cars to be used in the Royal procession were parked in the garage at the Macclesfield Arms Hotel quickly spread, and the visitors were so numerous that a barrier had to be erected round the cars to keep the crowds back. All the chief officials of the Corporation were out most of the day supervising the final arrangements. The Mayor was himself at the Town Hall for the greater part of the day. Late at night he made a final tour to see that everything was in order. Then, apart from those still engaged on the floral decorations, Macclesfield retired to bed to sleep. Many were up early. The great day had arrived!

Chestergate suitably bedecked for the Coronation.

119

19

Blackpool on Two Tin Trunks

"Barnaby fair, Barnaby bright, longest day and shortest night."

Countless sons and daughters of Macclesfield can look upon the annual Barnaby holiday with nostalgia. It was a time when the sun always seemed to shine and it was a time when everyone seemed to go to Blackpool. Macclesfield took over the seaside resorts of the north west of England in the last days of June and the first bit of July every year when all the mills, all the schools and all the shops closed down for the annual Barnaby holidays. How different now.

It was a time to be looked forward to through the long winter nights and the spring days. It was a time to save pennies and ha'pennies throughout the twelve months leading up to it and it was the time when the Co-op paid out the 'divi' just prior to the holiday. What a time. And when the vast majority of Maxonians had made their pilgrimage to the seaside a few stayed behind in a very empty town and a few stayed behind to clean the boilers in the mills. It was the only time during the entire year they were not in use.

Whenever I have written about those wonderful holidays there have been floods of letters in response. Take for instance the correspondence I received from Mrs Gibson of Wiltshire Close back in the late 1980s. She told me that in the early 1930s her later father, Harry Goodall, who was a well known haulage contractor in Macclesfield and a well respected man, made Barnaby holidays such fun. Many Maxonians must remember having their suitcases delivered in Blackpool on the morning they arrived. She wrote: "On the Friday night before

Barnaby started, people used to come to our house in Fence Street with their suitcases well labelled, where they had come from and their destination. Those who had tin trunks would be collected by my dad. It was two shillings for a suitcase and three shillings for a trunk.

Mr Frank Hargreaves kindly sent me this photograph taken in the early 1940s of Macclesfield people queuing at the bus station during Barnaby for their annual Blackpool holiday. In the photo is his father in law Sam Barber, well known local baker who had a shop in the Snow Hill area. Also in the picture is his foster son Bernard and three of his daughters, including Mr Hargreaves' late wife, Barbara, then Heather (now Perrin) and Marlene (now Wilson). Standing at the back is his son in law Derek Perrin.

She said a man called Harold Durrant who lived in Waterloo Street just around the corner always helped out with the luggage. Up would go the sheet rails on the lorry, then the sheet, making the vehicle waterproof. When all the suitcases were lined up in their order for delivery in their front room her dad would get out their little Morris 7 which in those days was the height of luxury and take her mum and elder sister to Blackpool. She was left behind to go with the luggage first thing Saturday morning. "We always stayed in the same private hotel in Albert Road every year" she recalled. Her dad would return

121

from Blackpool in the car and at first light on Saturday morning the lorry was all loaded up. "There were always two tin trunks placed at the tail-board end for myself and Harold to sit on. We used to sing at the top of our voices and Harold would whistle at all the girl cyclists as we went along."

On arrival in Blackpool she used to be dropped off first and then after breakfast her father and Harold would go and deliver everyone's luggage. More often than not their suitcase was waiting for them when they arrived off the crowded Barnaby Special train from Macclesfield. She and her family would be on the beach next day ready with buckets and spades.

Harold always took the lorry back home and she and her sister would always have a new blazer and canvas shoes, not forgetting the swim-suit and rubber ring. One evening was always kept aside to go to the Tower Ballroom for 5.30 p.m. to see the children's ballet. All the children were sat on the ballroom floor in a roped-off area and then afterwards Reginald Dixon would play the organ. She said: "It was a great night and afterwards we could go and look at the aquarium and the animals in the zoo. Although our hotel was quite a first class place we only had cold water at the wash-basin in our room so the landlady used to fill our hot water bottles at bedtime and next morning we used to use the same water to wash in.

After their week at Blackpool along would come Harold with the lorry and all the suitcases were collected again. This time her mother and sister went in the front of the lorry with her father and she and Harold sat on the tin trunks at the back. All the luggage was delivered back to the houses ... and it was a matter of waiting for next Barnaby.

A Silver Thrupenny Bit for the First to see The Tower ...

One person who vividly recalled to me, a few years ago, those days of Barnaby bright and fair was Harold Snape, a former resident of Macclesfield who went to live in Sale and then Blackburn.

Blackpool at Barnaby ... Mrs Betty Burgess (right) and friend Betty Cooke of Macclesfield around 1959. (J Burgess)

He wrote to me with his memories and I have much pleasure in giving them an airing within this book so those wonderful days will, once again, be so well remembered. Here they are:

"Macclesfield has something which, as far as I am aware, is quite unique and indeed unknown to any born more than five miles from its borders. This wonderful exciting time is called Barnaby, not "A Barnaby" or "The Barnaby". Just Barnaby.

"It, together with Christmas, was one of the two major events in the town life cycle. For Barnaby to this town is what Wakes is to Hindle or Oldham, it is the annual holiday, at one time a mere seven days but later a full 14.

"Even now I, a native of this town, find it difficult to conceive how anyone could stand two whole weeks of such excitement. For those unfortunates not having the advantage of being born in this ancient borough let me try to explain what Barnaby meant to a small boy in the 1930s.

"At Barnaby, most of the town's inhabitants went away and for those who stayed behind it was as though the whole corporate entity had pricked its finger and fallen fast asleep to await the kiss of a prince. Mills, both dark and satanic and light and airy, shops, factories, warehouses, and even some pubs closed and locked their doors. Little stirred, those left behind felt like intruders in their own town and looked furtively about as though guilty of some crime.

"At the time of which I speak, Macclesfield had two railway stations. Now, thanks to Dr Beeching, only one remains. Both stations were exciting to a small boy, one had a tunnel under the tracks which had a most satisfying echo when one shouted down, while the other had a long wooden floored inclined corridor which roared and clattered most agreeably when one ran up or down it. However, on Barnaby these pastimes faded into insignificance for outside both stations queues formed six deep for hundreds of yards, for the town was on the move.

"Men in their best flat caps stood by large cardboard suitcases containing their wives' holiday wear and wives in summer dresses guarded much smaller cases in which father's finery rested. Children clutched wooden spades and tin buckets, non-disposable items these, cared for since last Barnaby or even the one before that.

Blackpool at Barnaby ... Beryl Broadhurst, her niece Amy, Beryl's mum and Brenda Watkin. The tot at the front is Richard Watkin. (J. Burgess)

"There was no pushing or hard words, for these people were neighbours, workmates or drinking companions and nothing was gained by rushing – the railway companies were well aware of this annual migration and welcomed the extra revenue it brought. Extra trains were laid on and the extra trains had extra carriages, no one would be left behind, not at Barnaby, and the weather was always good. It never rained on Barnaby Saturday, or so it seemed to the boy.

"Strange conversations passed over his head, half heard but not forgotten. "Aye, he knows his crysants, won the Legion three years running." Or: "Doesn't surprise me, she always was a bit that way" another had recalled, but it was years before he understood. "In white as well, she should be ashamed, damned disgraceful.

"It was still before nine in the morning but this was no hardship for these people, for they would have been at their loom or bench for well over an hour on any other day but this.

"Eventually the station platform was reached but the boy rarely saw the great green and brass locomotive with its wonderful aroma of hot oil and steam, for here the crowd was dense and competition for a window seat in a smoking compartment was, if not fierce, at least jovially aggressive. To the boy it was a jungle of trousered legs, skirts and suitcases until Dad swung him up into the carriage and then heaved the heavy cases on to the luggage rack as though they weighed nothing at all. Dads could do things like that in those days, just as all Mams were infallible.

"The train slowly moved away and the boy could see over the gasworks wall, it looked quite different from the height of the bridge; and then the grammar school playing fields with its tiny figures in striped jerseys running about and he wondered why they too were not going away, feeling vaguely sorry for them. The train gathered speed, roaring through dark tunnels and village stations. Dad would say: "Look, son, here's Prestbury" and he would dutifully look at the flashing countryside. Each carriage had six sepia photographs for the travelling populace to stare at while being whisked about the country and the boy studied each in turn, slowly reading the captions below. "The Pavilion at Brighton" was one, it looked interesting, but where Brighton was he had no idea; it certainly wasn't in his town. Another was "The Kyles of Lochalsh" but no matter how long or hard he looked, he couldn't see Mr and Mrs Kyle among all that water.

"Then there were windows to breathe on so he could write his name or play noughts and crosses with Dad. Sometimes he would sit by his Mam and she would sing softly in time with the clackety clack of the rails. "We're on our way, we're on our way" keeping her lips close to his ear so other boys in the carriage wouldn't think he was soft. Later the same words would change to the same rhythm of the rails. "We're nearly there, we're nearly there." And Dad would call out: "A silver thruppenny bit for the first one to see the Tower!" and again the boy would press his nose against the cold hard glass of the window, even though he knew that whoever saw Blackpool Tower first he would still get a silver thrupennypiece – Dad would see to that.

YMCA members in Derby Street around 1946-47, before it was moved to Jordangate. The picture was taken opposite the club and includes a number of ladies from Ireland who came to Macclesfield after the war mainly to take up nursing at Macc. A number married and stayed in the area. Second row from the front on the left is Rose Readman, now Mrs K Simpson, who supplied the picture and now lives in Mottram St Andrew. Second from right is Ethel Cowell.

"Blackpool Station was enormous, a huge glass hall full of engines blowing off clouds of steam, porters in uniform pulling trolleys and most of the inhabitants of the town; and as the boy's father went through the barrier with a case in one hand, the boy in the other and the tickets in his teeth, people were calling to each other: 'See you in the Winter Gardens tonight' or 'Reg Dixon's on at The Tower again.'

"Some even took taxis, but the boy knew where he would be

staying, the same place as the last year and the year before. A mere half hour's walk from the sea, nothing to a boy whose Dad could make carrying heavy cases look so easy. Then the boarding house and he remembered last year when he had taken a bite from an apple on the sideboard to discover to his horror that it was made of wax and crumpled in his mouth and also his amazement when he found that they made the rice pudding in a washing up bowl two feet across. He wondered if he didn't bite any more wax apples perhaps they would let his scrape the skin from the edges of the great bowl.

"Of course, he would have to share a room again with Alec, the landlady's son, but as Alec went to school, even at Barnaby, he wouldn't see much of him.

"It was dinner time now and a week of visits to the zoo, the circus, the Fun House, Stanley Park, the piers and the beaches stretched out before him. How could it all be done in one week, even if that week was Barnaby?"

20

King's School Years & Scouting Days

Raymond Maddock now lives at Lyme Green. He will be known by many for his involvement with the local Scouting movement and he now lives in a house he designed and built as an ecological unit, making use of energy-saving systems.

Here he recalls his days at the King's School in the 1950s and his early days in the Macclesfield Scouts:

King's School Years

"Although I had been academically very bright at Athey Street School, my move to the King's School following success in the eleven plus examination came as a shock. Maybe I did not try enough but I always found myself competing for bottom place in the class with one D. Bailey. This experience does not seem to have hampered our progress in later life.

"As a new boy I remember T.T. Shaw was headmaster and he frequently arrived at assembly in carpet slippers. The head boy was then Dan Massey, a huge monster of a rugby player from Gawsworth. I well remember Nobby Clarke who taught us history, he still lives in Park Lane, not that I enjoyed history or was any good at it. Mr Harvey was deputy head and taught us French with little success. I was very good at Mathematics, my only good subject despite being taught by Mr Johnny Rushbrook. I often wonder if one is good at a subject because one likes it or does one like it because one is good at it? Two masters did teach me a lot. One was Mr Jardine who taught me metalwork and Mr Jones who's wife taught at the High School, and he taught me art. I recall he always referred to his pupils as bunny rabbits and when it snowed he came to school on skis.

T.T. Shaw, headmaster of the King's School, Macclesfield, for many years. He is pictured at Macclesfield High School's fair on May 25th, 1952, by Ray Maddock.

"The one master I owe the most to was Mr Burt who taught me English literature. I did not like the English literature but this six foot plus man organised the rambling club. Most weekends he would organise a hike for the sixth formers but myself, John Bradley and Howard Collier from the lower forth would regularly gate crash the outings. As a result I found that over the years I had walked just about every footpath within ten miles of Macclesfield. Three things stick in my mind about those hikes. One, we, that is, the three forth formers always walked well ahead of the main party. Two, our longest single hike was over a distance of 38 miles and we enjoyed every mile of it. The third and most vivid memory of our walks was that Mr Burt and the sixth formers always joked about the fact that in my packed lunch I always had a tin of rhubarb. I do not know why I did but I always did. I liked rhubarb and I never knew why the others thought it so funny.

"I did not like school very much. I played truant rather too much and I could not wait to leave and start work. We are always told that school days are the happiest days of your life. I would have agreed if I had not had to spend so many of them at school. There were many good things though, like playing on the rocks at lunch time, our versions of stone age cricket, using a stone and a branch of a tree, and waiting at the bottom of the field to catch the 1.10 p.m. train, the Comet, on its way to London.

"One thing always puzzled me about the King's School. While I was a pupil they erected large wrought iron gates at the main entrance to commemorate the war. There was pomp and ceremony at which we had to attend but from that day onward we, the pupils, were not allowed to use those gates. I never knew why.

Scouting Days

"From the age of eleven years, I found myself alternating between St John's in South Park Road and Newtown Methodists Sunday School in Hatton Street, depending on which had the best Christmas party or summer outing. I recall one trip where we were walked to the railway station in Macclesfield and taken by train to Bosley station from where we walked to a field behind the Queens Hotel on the A523 at Bosley. After playing games in the sun and eating jelly and ice cream along with potted meat sandwiches, we returned.

The Mayor's Sunday Parade in the Market Place. St John's Scout Band pictured outside the Parish Church in the early 1950s by Ray Maddock. Notice Redman's shop and Leach's Chemists and Hadfield's on the corner of Stanley Street.

"In the end I left both because neither had at that time a scout group, so I joined the 7th Macclesfield Brunswick troop which met at Brunswick Chapel in Chapel Street. The scoutmasters were Billy Richardson who had been in scouting since about 1907 along with Adam Hope, and Philip Tittensor. I was so enthusiastic that I had very soon been promoted to patrol leader of the Peewits, the other patrol being headed by Les Crone who later was to run the flower shop on Mill Lane where the end of the new by-pass now stands.

"As a small group they did not go camping but to my great joy we were invited to go to camp with the scouts of Sutton St

James. This was to be a week in North Wales just outside Bangor. I will always be grateful to George Foot for this my first experience of camping. On one particular day we had a great storm and the tent in which my patrol lived was badly torn and my first reaction was to go to George. He had enough problems of his own and swore at me and told me as patrol leader it was my problem. I went to the farm yard and found a large post and a maul, drove in the post and tied the tent to it and it survived the rest of the camp. It certainly taught me to do things for myself and not to rely on others. One of the finest lessons I ever learnt, thank you George.

St John's Scout Band on parade in Barton Street. (R Maddock)

Here's one to bring memories flooding back ... 'the stump', a favourite congregating place for local youngsters, in Leigh Street pictured in October of 1958. (G. Pownall)

"The rest of the camp was delightful. The driver of the train which crossed the viaduct on its way to Bangor always sounded his hooter and waved to us, while on the other side of the camp was a narrow gauge railway which carted slate from the quarries. We used to get a lift on this train up the line where we would cut firewood and the train on its way back would stop to pick up the wood and drop it off at the camp. I doubt safety regulations would not permit such a thing today.

"At the age of fifteen, I left Brunswick to join the newly formed group at St John's where the Scouters had never actually been scouts so I effectively became acting scoutmaster at fifteen. During my years at St John's I went to Gilwell Park for my wood badge and later represented England as a camp councillor in America. I helped the group and its band win every trophy available to it during the years I was there. There must be many men today who remember our camps abroad and our Gang Shows. The group still exists and the name over the door is still the one I gave the building, Mafeking Hall, following the parents committee purchase of the building when the church moved to Weston Estate. It seems like only yesterday. Mafeking Hall still stands and the new church on Weston is about to be demolished." (It now has been, and a new church erected.)

21

Notes on Music

Here is the second contribution to these pages, courtesy of the Dorey family, now living in Penzance. In it, Chris Dorey looks back on the musical scene of the 1950s – and much more ...

"When I went to work at 85 Chestergate, my father never uttered an adverse comment, though he knew for him it was the end of an era. As surely as the cat's whisker had twitched its last, so it was the end of the wireless, dry batteries and wet accumulators, which were the mainspring of his business. Hurdsfield born and bred, Fred Burke became the radio man of Bollington where he settled after marriage and we were always ready to leave our meals and favourite radio programmes to rescue someone whose battery had run out and even, if the occasion was important enough, lend them our own.

"Now it was radio by wire, the continuation of programmes was by stand-by receivers, boosted by six feet tall, valve filled giant amplifiers, deep in the cellars of Radio Relay on the corner of Westminster Street and Chestergate. Brain-child of Geoffrey Parker, landlord of the White Lion in Mill Street and ex BBC, and Alexander (Mac) McDougall, the intricate system comprised aerials on the roof and Nancy side, where the signal was excellent but subject to lightning strikes on occasion and receivers in the shop part of the building where subscribers paid their two-bob weekly fee – One and six O.A.P.s – for the service. The signal was set and maintained at a metered level and transmitted to thousands of homes in Macc and Bollington. My father, moving with the times, was incorporated on a freelance basis, supplying valves and effecting suitable repairs from his obsolete stock.

"From 6 a.m. when Ronnie Hutchins would open up, until midnight when Jack Riddell closed down, lines were checked for volume and distortion on a constantly operating line tester, specially designed by Mac, enabling any problems to be quickly located.

"Listening to the radio all day was my pleasant task though, as in the days when we missed crucial parts of our programme to supply batteries, we now had to check all four lines: Light, Home, Third and Foreign stations at regular intervals.

"It was the quality radio of the '50s, though Radio Relay was precisely that – a relay of broadcast material – and was not licensed to broadcast live, except for local police messages. However, the staff was kept busy on the phone and in the shop, with updates of the latest scores in big sporting events.

"After the announcement of the death of King George VI, no music was allowed to be relayed for a suitable period of mourning, as dictated by the BBC.

"With speakers home based and linked by wire directly to Radio Relay, the streets were free of the impact of modern-day ghetto blasters.

"P.A. systems were loaned for many functions and were regularly used by the many musicians at that time, whose excellence could have earned them a broadcasting or recording slot. From the old Paragon and Bronc Read bands, plus a few others, was formed the prize winning Regionaires Big Band, its tremendous rendering of Ray Noble's *Cherokee* gained it a three-year contract at Dukinfield Town Hall in the face of fierce competition. Not surprising with Albert Brodie on drums, Jack Jordan on bass, Maurice Davenport and Harold Barnet trumpets, Jim Butterworth trombone and Bert Cordon, Ken Davies, Ron Lomas and Vernon Fitchett on saxes and clarinets. Les Riseley, music teacher and St Andrew's choir master was on piano. Vocals were shared between Albert and me, though I lost my job on the lights. Playing for effect, red for *She Wears Red Feathers* and blue for *Blue Moon*, was thought very appropriate, until they played *Dancing in the Dark*, when my zeal proved too much for them to read their band parts.

Opposite: This photograph of lady covenanters outside the Gospel Hall in Derby Street should bring back some memories. It was above the premises occupied by Avery Scales and it later moved and became Carisbrook Chapel. The picture was taken, most probably, around the years leading to the Second World War, by Miss Rene Wildgoose, a teacher at Mill Street school. Pictured (back row, standing, left to right): Annie Gosling, Annie Walker, Vera Walker, Mrs Leach, Ann Thornley, Ruth Hand, Mary Henshall, Lena Tomlinson, Alice Tomlinson, Elsie Richardson, Miss Edith Wildgoose. Seated: Joyce Houghton, Jessie Yates (nee Hurstfield) with shield, Alice Warren.

"Later I joined the Banjo, Mandolin and Guitar Club, which at that time met in The Commercial Hotel in Brook Street. John Trafford, who had spent some of his time in Hawaii in the RAF and had collected much of their traditional music, formed the Kalima Trio with himself on steel guitar, accompanied by the ukuleles of Bill Cleaver and Fred Slack. My love of and ability to sing in Hawaian, found me a place as their vocalist and we did cabaret plus charity work, including on one bitter winter night, the T.B. ward at Moss Lane Hospital, with me in my grass skirt – and the windows wide open. We also appeared in the first round of the inter-town talent contest but as grass skirts did not make good maternity wear I retired before the second round.

"Although 'Hodgsons, the record shop' was still in the Market Place the Chestergate camaraderie had a music all its own for those who worked there. It was a real neighbourhood and often as I walked to work, after a friendly smile to the policeman on point duty on Boots' corner, more friendly if he was young and good looking, Mr Rowley, champion coffee roaster of Pott and Thompson would bob out of the shop with a neatly-folded packet of his newest blend for me to try. Claudia Sheldon would also wave me in to see the latest addition to her collection of bird miniatures and George Hill would lean out to tell me of a new delivery of Clarkes shoes, my style and size, he was always right and I never went into that shop to select a pair of shoes.

"I was always welcome at number 78, the paper shop belonging to Tom Raw, his wife and son George, who was a fine cricketer for Macclesfield. When it was the Newsagents Ball in 1954 I was invited to stay the night, for though I was educated and worked in Macc I still lived 'Up Cross' in Bollington. George

was booted out of his room and went to stay with his friend, George Billington, who stood each morning at the top of Hibel Road station slope, handing newspapers to the regular and just as regularly last minute train travellers. The most unmusical sound to my ears was George's alarm clock going off only a couple of hours after I'd gone to bed. It was one of those raucous things designed to get him up without fail, to collect the day's papers from the early train and he'd forgotten to switch it off – or knowing George, perhaps he didn't forget.

"I didn't know then that the boy I'd met at the Ball was to become my husband a year later and that he was the son of the previous Paragon Dance Band drummer Walter Dorey.

"Les Riseley, looking very angelic, played the organ at our wedding but had warned me he was going to 'swing it' when I was half way up the aisle, enough to make any bride nervous.

"Also in 1954 John Barbirolli came to the Drill Hall in Bridge Street with the Hallé Orchestra, a rare and enjoyable experience. The Drill Hall was accustomed to music, for it was here the 25th Macclesfield Detachment of Army Cadets rehearsed the Corps of Drums, which in the early seventies swept the board for several years, by winning best band, drum major and with our son winning the Silver Trumpet as champion trumpeter of Cheshire; this enabled him to play at remembrance services and the band to parade around the town, setting a pace for the Macc Carnival, which had the little legs of carnival queen attendants and the like, moving in a blur of white ankle socks."

The music scene is all changed now, news of what's on and opinions on performance all appear in the Macc Express. Mostly we listen at home; by wireless once more. No more linked together by underground cable or under-eave wiring stapled up for a peppercorn rent. For that personal, Old Maxonians' togetherness you have to be ill in hospital with the volunteers of Bedside Radio.

Still, the melody lingers on, even if the manuscript is filed away in the archives. Tied with silk ribbon, of course.

Macclesfield Jazz Club

Meetings every *THURSDAY* at the
STANLEY HALL ANNEXE
at 7-45 p.m.

•

Appearing at ALL Club Sessions

Our own Resident Jazz Band—
THE SILKTOWN STOMPERS

Membership **2/6** *per Year*

Weekly
Meetings - **1/-**

★ EVERY THURSDAY EVENING real Jazz will be heard at the STANLEY HALL ANNEXE! Arrangements are being made to obtain well-known Jazz Recitalists as guests of the club, and the first one, who on Thursday, 20th March, will give a record recital to the club called "An Outline of Jazz," is that ever-popular Secretary of the Manchester Jazz Club . . .

JACK GREGORY

. . . who may be described as one of the authorities on Jazz in the country, so don't miss the FIRST (or any other) meeting of—at last—Macclesfield's own Jazz Club! Come along and enjoy your jazz in ideal surroundings and have a gossip, over a cup of coffee and a cake, with people who have the same interests as yourself, and listen to the discussions and arguments so beloved by all jazz followers

We should
be pleased to see
YOU
next Thursday !

If you are a real JAZZ lover
you are urged to join now—
TO-NIGHT !

Macclesfield Jazz Club ... a poster showing the resident band was the Silktown Stompers.
(C. Dorey)

Remember the Cavendish Coffee Bar and Jones Music Stores in Queen Victoria Street? (Mrs Rumsay).

Staff of Mowbrays pictured in the late 1950s. The premises were in King Edward Street in the building taken over by Macclesfield Rural District Council and the company later moved to Hurdsfield.

The year is 1954 and Macclesfield postmen Philip and Colin Swindells (brothers) and Arthur Beresford line up at the Castle Street premises, later taken over by the Cheshire Building Society. The photograph was supplied by David Swindells, himself a postman, whose wife, Nichola, is also a postwoman. Colin Swindells may be best known nowadays as secretary of the Prince Albert Angling Society.

The Bridgewater Arms dominoes and darts teams in the 1950s. In the picture kindly supplied by Mrs Cotterill are Jack Fieldtead, Norman Dale, Harry Hancox, Frank Clare, Denis Potts, Robert Robertson, David Burgess, Ernie Nield, Alec Robertson, Ernie Swan, Norman Sutton, and 'Jigger' Wood.

22

The Corner Shop –
Oasis of the Borough

It is now a good number of years since I first had the pleasure of meeting Harry Williamson. Many will know Harry for his articles in the Macclesfield Express on his childhood days and, later, his early working days at a solicitor's office in King Edward Street. Later he became a grocer and during that time delved into the history of his corner shop – a place he describes as 'The Oasis of the Borough'. Here is his story:

"I would, at first, like to ask a question: Can you identify the shop premises which has for 171 years sold, amongst many other goods, one item continuously? A clue or two may assist: Firstly, it's a retail business on a main road; secondly it could have been owned by the Arkwright family, and thirdly, the answer is a four letter word. The solution will appear in due course. If further help is needed, I must emphasise this is not a long standing family business, such as Hadfields, Chemist and Drysalters, or Hankinsons the Bakers. These two families have given service to the Macclesfield public for a joint total of over four hundred years. From conception their assistance to local life has been – and still is – par excellence.

"Hadfields commenced trading in the Market Place in 1755, and in the passage of time were involuntarily moved to number one Mill Street, at that time the residence of the business's owner, because their original shop was demolished by public order. During my lifetime number one Mill Street became a Mecca for the population of the town. The shop appeared to sell everything from A to Z in its fields of operation, one long-serving member of its staff had a great personality and sense of humour – that gentleman was Stan Hough. He was an outstanding asset to the Chemist and Drysalter.

"Writing the name of 'Stan Hough' immediately brought the recollection of another well-known local figure, Peter Wardle, Haulage Contractor, originally of Edward Street, who in the 1920s had two steam-engine wagons which were parked close to the skating rink in Prestbury Road. These machines were the largest producers of bleach in the northern hemisphere. In my childhood my trousers produced evidence in support of this allegation.

"Peter Wardle was always like my second father and he told me a couple of stories about, as he put it, " 'Adfields", the first tale commenced while Peter was being served by Stan, and unfortunately one item was out of stock, something like the following conversation took place:

Peter: "When ar't going gerra it?

Stan replied: "Ah Dunna know. It met be next wick.

Peter retorted: "S'laf go to ah dacent shop.

Stan then invited his customer to go to warmer climes.

Peter replied: "Nay, ah'm not non going therr, onny tha' grandad or th'dad ud serve me off 'is shovel. Ah'll cum in nex' wick an' thee must knock summat off.

Stan opened the door and said goodbye with these words: "Beggar off an' cum in on Wensdye.

"This incident did not stop Peter Wardle remaining an advertising agent for " 'Adfields". He would extol the virtues of what he called " 'Adfields 'Orse Hoil". His pronunciation of the word 'horse' produced some misunderstandings as to where the solution should be applied, most listeners thought it meant to the lower lumber regions of the spine. When questioned Peter replied: "Norra at'al. I rubbed some inter back of an owd nag I 'ad, and th'day after me missus said she were a lot berra.

"Hadfields were forced to move again under compulsory purchase when the Grosvenor Shopping Centre was instigated and they now trade in Churchill Way.

"I have now 'run outer bread', so I must go to the bakers, but before I do, I must mention that while researching the history of Macclesfield, I was amazed to discover that in 1815 one member from each of the Hadfield and Hankinson families joined together in an attempt to introduce gas street lighting into the darkness of Mill Street. They failed, both losing a lot of money. No doubt Mr Hadfield found some ointment to sooth both his and Mr Hankinson's burnt fingers.

The 'Oasis' of Macclesfield: Harry Williamson's grocery shop.

"In 1820 the Hankinson family opened their bakehouse in Mill Street adjacent to what is now the Majestic Cinema, moving in 1888 to Adlington Street, from which they departed in 1918 to their present premises in Coare Street. One hundred and seventy four years service to the local public is outstanding. There must be many reasons for this continuity. One particular circumstance springs to mind: Some years ago when the national bakers went on strike, more than once, Hankinson's present owner, Geoff, worked over 20 hours a day to supply his customers, that is a fact.

"Hankinson's supplied bread to my shop for over thirty years. Long before I had business connections with Geoff, our parents had been friends from their school-days. Whenever our fathers met in their days of manhood they would settle all the world's problems and increase the brewers' profits considerably.

"In 1823 part of Macclesfield Common, known as Gallows Field, was made available on 999 year leases to several applicants. A gentleman named Barber secured a corner plot in Broken Cross Lane, that thoroughfare being re-christened Chester Road in 1824. Mr Barber was a blacksmith. His intentions were, no doubt, to open a smithy on the, then, outskirts of the town. He also had the brilliant idea of brewing beer to sell to his customers while they waited for their horses to be shod; the liquid was better received than red-hot horse shoes so he shoved the anvil "up Shadys weskit" and concentrated on brewing. A wise and far sighted decision. (All my intelligent readers will, by now, have identified the glorious four-letter word – BEER!)

"When Mr Barber opened his premises, what public services were available in Macclesfield? Houses had no water, sewage, gas or electricity installed. No railway or canal, no public transport other than the stage-coach, no Police Force or Member of Parliament. By modern standards in the words of the comic song, 'Nothing to laugh at – at all'.

"Most streets were un-made, mud and sludge would be enemies to the clogs and bare feet of the locals, particularly in the winter. However, one man's loss is another man's gain. The farming fraternity of Gawsworth, Henbury, Pexhill and possibly Siddington and Marton would come to Chestergate, Jordangate and the Market Place trying to dispose of their produce.

"As the town had no public lighting, about two o'clock in the dark season, they would metaphorically speaking 'put up their shutters' to commence a long walk home. But what about un-sold stock? The living standards of the farmer depended on

Market Day sales. Someone had the bright idea of calling on Mr Barber, at what had become number 82 Chester Road, and bartering vegetables, chickens, rabbits and eggs for cash or beer. I'll bet a 'bob' that, in a buyer's market, Mr Barber got cartloads of goods for a pint of ale, or under pressure, maybe two. Without the non-existent Town and Country Planning Committees approval he entered the grocery field, his candle and oil lamp lit shop was open almost 100 hours a week. Now we are almost back to square one!

Before supermarkets came to town it was personal service for each and every customer. There were many stores around Chestergate and Mill Street that could supply everything you needed in the grocery and provision lines – and would deliver to your door as well. This picture was provided by Mr and Mrs W.E. Rhodes of Hurdsfield. Mr Rhodes was manager at the Home and Colonial for many years and I know a lot of people remember him from those times. Mrs Rhodes also worked for many years behind the counter at the stores. Pictures are Home and Colonial staff behind the counter around 1950, left to right: Mr W.E. Rhodes (manager), father and son Jack and Barry Longden, Joan from Rushton, Miss Prince, Sheila Archer, Doris Hicks.

"Successive generations of the Barber family ran the shop until the mid-1880s when they sold out to the local brewers W.A. Smith & Son Ltd. The brewers installed tenants who, by written agreement, paid rental and rates and must purchase all alcoholic stocks from the brewery. Failure to do so resulted in the tenant putting " 'is 'at and coat on" and leaving the oasis to walk into the dessert.

"Smiths owned the premises until 1960 when I, the existing tenant, after some long and hard negotiations, purchased the property and became independent. During the years of the brewer's ownership there were quite a number of tenants, the longest serving of whom were the Lowry family, a mother and two daughters. They reigned at number 82 for more than thirty years. In their period of office the off-licence area was known as the 'Bottle and Jug' department; every time a customer required draught beer one of these ladies, with jug in hand, descended the cellar steps to measure and supply the order. The cellar steps were of stone, human feet had worn each step arc-shaped; they could only be equalled with their counter-points in the mediaeval towers of Caernarvon Castle in Wales. (Speaking of Wales, most Macclesfield shopkeepers had to do business with the Slate Merchants for an awful lot of their clients had their purchases 'put on the slate' until next Friday!) The shop was partitioned, had two entrances, one in Chester Road and the other in Adlington Street (called the side door). This way of entry was known as 'Teetotallers Road of Admission'. Lucy, of the Lowry family, joined my staff part-time, when Burdins, where she was then working, closed down. Lucy regaled me with many amusing stories of her previous Chester Road lifetime appertaining to TTs. One I recollect in particular is of a gentleman who poked his nose around the door, breathed a sigh of relief if the shop was empty, produced two empty Guinness bottles from his raincoat's capacious pockets and would say: "Swop 'em quick" continuing with "They are not for me. I've a friend coming tonight and unfortunately he drinks." Miss Lowry would laugh saying "He'd more drinking pals than I've had good dinners, he came every night and twice on Sunday.

"The drinking of stout, such as Guinness and Mackeson, seemed to me to have a profound effect on the longevity of many OAPs. Their life-span often exceeded the late 80s and 90s. Now I have joined the group of senior citizens, I have the constant worry that I don't like the stuff!

"When I was appointed 'Head Arab' of the oasis on the 11th August 1958, I returned to the Victorian Age. The shop floor was unevenly stone flagged; behind the counter duck-boards were in situ, walking on them required the skill of a circus acrobat. The time that I was carrying four trays of eggs and stumbling on the duck-boards I catapulted 120 chickens' creations into the window will stay in my mind until my dying day (which, without stout, will be sooner rather than later). I stood in shock and bewilderment. It was no yoke. The boss (my wife) arrived at the scene of the disaster – she described her husband's capabilities in a forthright manner. Under feminine instructions I immediately followed in voluntary terms to clean up the mess. My eggo (I mean ego) was deflated.

One of the many corner shops in Macclesfield: Billington's newsagents at the corner of King Street and Buxton Road. (G Pownall)

"In an attempt to gain additional patronage in 1960, the shop was completely renovated from floor to ceiling. It cost two arms, two legs and the remaining hair on a bald-headed looney. Associated with the theory, which cost nowt, that if a customer departed with a smile on their face they almost certainly returned. A smile and a laugh had to be the shop's trademark. Another very important factor in relation to No 82's long life

151

must be its situation, in the local neighbourhood. It was called 'the Top Shop', regretfully in real terms that is a geographical description, Chester Road, Crompton Road and Adlington Street all rise to the shop's entrances. In a lighter vein the premises had other nick-names – 'a gold mine' – always having been in the ownership of the descendants of 'Robbing Hood' who took from the poor and fed himself richly.

Hurdsfield Road: in the thirties and forties the shop pictured was Mr Fred Drinkwater's 'Little Favourite' shop selling groceries and grain. The van in the picture is obscuring what used to be Rushton's Chippie. (G Pownall)

"There are a 1001 stories waiting to be told about the oasis, which in 1988 was acquired by the Portland Wine Co Ltd, the reason for this change was simple, I was taken ill and without taking the hump, I was placed on a medical camel and escorted from the hallowed spot, blinkin 'eck!

"One final afterthought ... I have resolved to start 'supping stout' to lengthen the time of my personal happy memories of 'th shop ont' corner."

152

23

More Sweet Memories

So popular was Muriel Oakes' contribution to the last book 'So Well Remembered' that I had no hesitation in asking her for another (and it was also a good excuse to have a cuppa and a home-made biscuit with her at the same time!) What better way of almost concluding this book, I thought, than a Muriel Oakes poem!

From her collection of amusing ditties she produced the following, which we both agreed was just the ticket. Muriel's 'naughty but nice' style of poetry has entertained hundreds upon hundreds, but she did think it necessary to explain a few phrases. 'Caught on the change' meaning 'pregnant on the menopause' and 'everything taken away' being a 'full hysterectomy'. I know most senior Maxonians will be aware that 'ess hole' was the back of the fire where the ashes were and 'Uncles' was the pawn broker.

Anyway, here is Muriel's poem:

Now language was different, when we were all young,
To foreigners, it would sound strange
What would they have said if they'd heard someone say,
"Our Lisa's got caught on the change".

We would stand in the yard, trying so hard to hear,
And pretending that we were at play.
And then we would hear the most terrible news,
"She's had everything taken away!

When they bought something new, it was quite an event,
They would ponder then put down a deposit,
And that place in the yard, well, it wasn't a loo,
It was known to us all as the closet.

A little black figure would come staggering out,
nd the kids would shout, "Look at our Ben",
Then the mother would say, "I've told him till I'm sick",
He's been up the ess-hole again".

The young men were so smart in their lovely best suits,
Like peacocks they were on a Sunday,
It didn't last long for the suits were wrapped up
And taken to 'Uncles' on Monday.

Thursday night was the time all the cleaning was done,
We worked so hard we deserved a big trophy,
The fire irons were polished, put away till week end,
They were tucked underneath the old 'sofy'.

When a baby was born, it was no great big deal,
There was never a banner or a flag,
The children were told (we believed it as well)
Nurse Clark fetched it round in a bag.

The house at the corner they had so many kids,
The father he sure had the knack,
The youngest would say, "Nurse Clark brought you here,
Well, couldn't she take this one back".

When Barnaby came the excitement was there,
There were queues down the Hibel Road Station
They planned all their holidays one year to the next,
Cos no one had heard of inflation.

When the kids broke a window they had nightmares for weeks,
They daren't vandalise for a hobby,
If they were found out then they got their desserts,
A clip round the ear from the Bobby!

154

There was always a woman who knew what to do,
If a child was off colour or sick,
She told the child's mother, "No messing about",
Now get a good road through him, quick.

When Friday came round it was bath night again,
The tin bath by the fire to step in,
The right side of your body all red from the fire,
The left, rigor mortis set in.

Underprivileged we were but we didn't know,
As a word we'd have thought it quite funny,
We were all quite content, everyone was the same,
And nobody had any money.

But we'd something more precious no money could buy,
Although life was such a hard grind,
Old folks went to bed with their back doors unlocked,
Cos everyone had peace of mind.

It was such an event when a mill girl got wed,
She was proud of the ring on her finger,
And some had a posser and some had a tub.
But the richest of all had a wringer.

So God bless all the people in Macclesfield town,
Life's different now, lots more pressure,
But I will think we're lucky to live where we are,
And it must be the best town in Cheshire.

24

Wars, Ghosts and
a Pinch of Snuff

Just as I was preparing this book for publication, Mrs Amy
Stuart of Minor Avenue, Lyme Green, visited me with these
memories. We got to talking about the fact that names like
'Amy' are now coming back into fashion – everything goes full
circle. Anyway, here are her recollections:

"I always remember my late mother-in-law telling me about
when she was a young woman, standing outside the Barracks
in Crompton Road and watching the soldiers going off to the
Boer War.

"One of my vivid memories is of the Victory Parade after the
Second World War. We went and stood outside the Co-op in
Park Lane, across from Dobson and Thornhills butchers. The
incident that stands out in my mind – down Park Lane, the
Yanks (as we called the American soldiers) who I think were
billeted at the Drill Hall in Bridge Street; every dinner time they
would march down Park Lane to go to Lord Street for their
meals. Well, back to the Victory Parade down Park Lane. The
Yanks came marching down in their sloppy fashion as usual .
Of course the crowd gave them a good clap and cheered them
on their way. Next were the 'Cheshires' and a woman ran into
the road waving and shouting "what about a cheer for our own
lads!" What a sight for sore eyes. They were so smart and
efficient and marched in precision as always. You never heard
such a cheer go up from the crowd. I can still weep at the
thought of it. I felt so proud of them.

"The next incident a few years ago was the Parade down Mill

Street after a ceremony for them in the Market Place. There was no one hardly on the Green but what a sight to see. Tears rolled down my cheeks. How proud I felt standing there watching. What went through my mind at the time. Why didn't they arrange for the school children to line up to see them pass by. It was a sight worth watching. I have always felt proud to be born and live in Macclesfield and on my travels I have always, when asked where I came from, been proud to say Macclesfield, Cheshire.

A school photograph that is sure to get memories working overtime ... Byron Street School about 1920. (Mrs A. Oliver)

"I remember the cabs and black horses outside St Peter's Church at funerals. But as far back as I can remember, going round with my Aunt to see the dead people in their coffins. What a little ghoul I must have been, but it was a way of life then. Neighbours used to help wash the dead. Many a time there would be a knock on our door for my mother to go and lay them out, as it was called. Also she used to help at births as well. Then they used to send for Joe Lowe and Nurse Clark respectively. Then after going to the interment at the Cemetery, the mourners used to go home and have currant bread and oatcakes and cheese and plenty of tea to wash it down.

"On going one day to the bus station with my mother and her friend who was very droll, we passed Joe Lowe's. In the window was a pot with the name of the person and age 91. Liza said to my mother, "Nipped int' bud". I could not understand what she meant till years after it came to me.

Snuff Taking

"When I was quite small, a lot of women used to take brown stuff. They kept it in a small Coleman's mustard tin. A lot of the silk workers used to have a pinch, maybe off some of the others. They kept it in a little pocket under their aprons with snuff-rags. It was banned in the mills and I knew one woman who was sacked at Frost's Mill for having snuffy ends on the silk. It was banned in our house by my father, but my Aunt, who lived with us, used to hide hers in a safe place. I don't remember any women who smoked cigarettes in those days but plenty who 'knocked the box'. My Aunt used to call it Laudanum. The grocers' shops used to stock it and you could buy half an ounce. The shopkeepers were instructed not to sell it to children. It must have been very anti-social. I once sneaked a pinch and sneezed my head off. The regular users never used to sneeze at all.

Ghost Stories

"In the back yard of about 18 houses a wall across the bottom was what we called 'the big flag'. It was a very large, flat stone wall with a hole at one end. I think it must have been what we used to call a big slopstone, the old name for the sink. We were always cleaning it and Donkey stoning it, or a white stone, round the edges. Well, in the school holidays after a day of play we used to gather on the 'big flag' (we used to call the pavements flags). The young children used to say "tell us a story Amy" and we used to huddle there in the dusk and I used to make it up as I went along, all sorts of blood curdling events and ghosts.

158

"Then towards the end it would be dark and I used to jump up and say there was a ghost and run down the entry with a gang of kids screaming at the back of me. But they enjoyed it. Even now I get stopped in the street and told how they used to enjoy the ghost stories I used to tell.

"Brasshouse Street and Copper Street smelt houses all must have had some significance, and over the foundry. The Rose Inn stood at the bottom of Brasshouse Street, kept by Joe Sherratt. Then there was a slope and a flight of steps, a row of houses with gardens and down the steps were a few red brick houses by the railway wall. We used to go and swing on the gates at the crossings till the signal man ran us off. One night the house at the end of the row at the top of the steps (the kitchen window was nearly level with the footpath as it was built on the slope) well, the window was cracked and had a hole in it. We were passing by and saw Mr. B shaving himself by candlelight, so we blew the candle out and were chased by Mr B brandishing his cut-throat razor. The window was mended soon after that.

"Also, here lived a poor family who used to make a living by poaching rabbits, and you would see them sat on the wall with their large pockets full of nets, waiting for the moon either to go in or out – I never knew.

"Some days during the holidays, we used to go and play on the clay 'bonc' at the bottom of Windmill Brew, or Brow. There used to be a line of posts with iron bars running through and the children used to tipple over doing the 'sheep hang', just tippling over and hanging just by their legs. Some of the girls were very clever and used to do all sorts of tricks on the bars, never me – I could only go backwards and not forwards. Then the small children would be digging the clay and making all sorts of objects with it.

"I always used to be taking the children out of the Square on walks, mostly up the Hollins and down to Langley and a dog or two would join us. We always had a dog at home. Then one or two more would see us going and ask if they could come. We always used to take bottles of water with us. By the time we reached the top of Richmond Hill we had drunk most of the water and used to call at Mrs Hargreaves who very kindly used to refill our bottles. She used to make lovely home-made ginger beer etc but it was never too much trouble for her to fill our bottles. Sometimes we used to go into Mitchells field to make daisy-chains but if he saw us he would chase us off.

Knight Street with Birchenough's bakehouse at the bottom, October 1958. (G Pownall)

"First field, second field and third field, mostly taken over by golfers now. We always had to be careful of the golfers as it was dangerous, then after the third field we would go up Noe's Hill. We used to call it Noah's Hill. A good place for blackberrying, then down into the last two fields to Langley Road. We used to go in the wood to pick bluebells or wood anemones. Then right down the road to Byrons Lane. We used to run past one house in Byrons Lane that was supposed to have had a murder done in it. Fighting with red hot pokers was the story. Over Gunco Lane, sometimes we would stand on the window sill to watch the women who worked at Backhouse and Coppack's catching the paper. Then over the foundry and past Carlisle's Mill and pond, or pool. Children were warned not to go near the pool as there was a whirlpool in the middle, but I swam across it one hot day and proved it was not a whirlpool. I was quite a tomboy in those days, climbing walls and whatnot.

Good Fridays

"We used to walk in Prestbury fields and paddle in the Bollin, eat our 'bucks' as we used to call our bread and jam. Drink our water that we used to take in bottles of course. Play games and dry our feet on the grass. Then came the treat. We saved our tuppences and walked to Prestbury Station and booked our seats to Macclesfield. What a thrill when we went under the tunnel and the lights came on. How we used to cheer. Then into Hibel Road Station. I think that was the main station, I never remember using the Central Station much. We often stood in the long queues at Barnaby week to go to Blackpool. We used to go Monday till Friday as it was cheaper mid-week. We used to stay in Albert Road. There were nearly all Macc folk staying there. Mother used to collect tins of food for weeks before and she used to pack it into straw cases, one used to fit inside the other, and then fastened with leather straps round. She never used to Board as it was called, that was for folks with plenty of money. Every day the landlady used to come round and ask us what we wanted for meals. Then at the end of our stay she would present the bill and at the bottom she used to put a charge for the 'cruet'.

"Mother used to work in the silk at Frost's and she was a thrifty housekeeper and good cook. She could make a meal out of next to nothing. We always had good suppers, cheese and onions thickened in a sauce to dip our bread in. I used to have to go in Mill Lane for twopenn'orth of cheese bits from Allen's – all the crumbs on the board after cutting the cheese. I remember people going into Allen's and they used to let you taste the cheese off the end of a knife, nearly two ounce. I don't know where my father got the cheese, but I have seen many a half of a cheese on a shelf in the kitchen. But what a pong it was, what we called rotten cheese. It used to smell the house out. It was a family treat and they used to cook it in front of

161

the fire in what was called a Dutch Oven. We used to have a kind of shelf that used to fit on the bars of the fire. Then the Dutch Oven was placed on it and the cheese used to be on the bottom and maybe sausages or bacon used to hang on the hooks and all the fat would drip down onto the cheese. Then the cheese and the fat would all go creamy and with a skitter of pepper it made a lovely meal to dip our bread in. Then back to the suppers. Mother would ask me to go in the lane again to the tripe shop where I used to have to ask for twopenn'orth of tripe pieces. Pieces that had been trimmed off the tripe. Then with a couple of big onions mother would cook a delicious dish of tripe and onions in a brown dish, when you opened the over door it was all bubbling up, mmmm! I must tell you, as I was growing up I wasn't keen on going for tripe pieces so then I hit on the idea of asking for tripe parings. It seemed better. Then when the broad beans were in season mother would get a thick piece of bacon. Thickened and stewed in the oven, they were delicious. My father used to have an allotment and provided the beans. He also used to keep pigs somewhere along Black Road. In the winter we used to have steak and cow-heel pie with a crust on it – delicious, and pea soup with pigs feet or a ham bone. Then we would have a cows heart, roasted. Sheep's jimmy (head) made lovely soup, and the brains mashed up, and when I was little I used to try to get the teeth out of the jaw bone. As I got older I was learning science etc at the Central School for Girls and all about the heart and the way it worked. I didn't want to eat it anymore. Mother always had a pan on the fire cooking something.

"I remember Ben Wragg's shop in Mill Lane nex to Victoria Arch. He used to sell a lot of cheap meat. The poor people used to go a lot. He used to sell 'Shilling Lapups'. They used to be all wrapped up and you didn't know what you were getting till you got home. I heard some people call them 'Rhapsodies in Blue'. My brother used to say "Is this from Ben Wragg's?" and mother would deny it or else he wouldn't have eaten it. Mother, at one time, used to bake her own bread and I used to see the dough rising in a warm place near the fire and sometimes she made her own jam, and went to work full time as well, bless her.

The continually changing face of Macclesfield ... not so very long ago, before the Silk Road was built, this arch was a well known landmark in Mill Lane. It led to the Victoria Mills, so the plaque in the wall says, and was constructed in 1837. (Picture A Rowbotham, Clarke Terrace)

Penny Crush

"Saturdays were good days. Mother used to send my older brother and me to get my father's wages. He was a blacksmith and used to work in, I think, 'The Flying Horse' yard, it was once called. If we had not gone for his money he would have gone into one of the pubs and spent the lot as was very common in those days. My mother said, don't come home without her share, then he could go where he liked. Those great big shire horses used to be shod, lovely big gentle creatures. But the size of them was frightening to me, a tiny girl.

"Well, now we come to the exciting part of Saturday. Clutching our pennies in our hands we either used to call at Fitzjohn's at the bottom of Duke Street (a little man with a hooked nose) for fruit, or we would call at Hewitt's fruit shop on the right-

163

hand side of Mill Street. I think it belongs to Jackson's bread shop now. Anyway, we used to buy a tuppenny bag of damaged fruit. Then we used to get in the large queue in Duke Street at The Palace, later called The Regal. Now it is no longer used. It was a penny to go in and we used to sit on the wooden forms. The orchestra was situated behind a green velvet curtain hanging from brass rings. Then it was nearly time for the film to start. By the way, they were silent. Usually cowboys and Indians, Tom Mix and Tony (his horse). A man who used to play on one of the musical instruments had a bald head, and the boys used to throw damaged fruit at him, poor fellow. Then the lights would dim and the cowboys and Indians would start. Booing and cheering from the lads and girls, you can imagine the state of the 'Bug Hut' (as it was affectionately called). Damaged fruit all over the floor! Nearly all the children had what was known as a 'Friday's Penny', the lucky ones, that is. People used to go on the stage. At one time they used to have 'Joy Nights' and there would be prizes.

The Baths

"What a thrill we got out of going to the Baths in Davenport Street from school to learn to swim. Hackneys were the managers. Then Mr Booth after them. They used to have lines across with rings on and they used to pull you across. Having first had you all lay on the boards out of the cabins teaching you your strokes. Then in turns you would get in one of the rings and they used to pull you across the bath doing your strokes, or trying to.

"The cabins were all round the sides with canvas curtains on rings. We always used to try and get the corner cabins, which were doubles. We would take our sandwiches to eat afterwards as it made you hungry with all the exercise. The girls baths had all white slippery tiles, but the boys had a new one with a cork surface at the bottom. They used to hold their swimming galas there. I took part in quite a few but never could beat Millie Garside, who couldn't be beaten in those days!

"The girls always had to wear a swimming hat, and you always had to wash your feet in the showers before you went in the water. As I got older I used to go to the baths on Saturday mornings. We only had a limited time in the water, then every now and again Lily Hackney would come and blow a whistle and shout you to come out. We would go and hide in the double cabins and then Lily would go out for a while, so we used to come out and dive back into the water again, or another ruse was to change our coloured caps. We used to stay in the water till all our fingers were crinkled with staying in the water too long. Then we would eat our soggy sandwiches and go home."

Remember Royles Terrace like this? (G Pownall)

Premier OATCAKE, MUFFIN & CRUMPET BAKER.

SHOPS SUPPLIED TO ANY DISTANCE.

11 Prestbury Road, Macclesfield.

We publish guides to individual towns, plus books on walking and cycling in the great outdoors throughout England and Wales.
This is a recent selection:

Local Guidebooks

CHESHIRE: its magic and mystery – Doug Pickford *(£6.95)*

STAFFORDSHIRE: its magic and mystery – Doug Pickford *(£6.95)*

PORTRAIT OF MACCLESFIELD – Doug Pickford *(£6.95)*

PORTRAIT OF MANCHESTER – John Creighton *(£6.95)*

PORTRAIT OF STOCKPORT – John Creighton *(£6.95)*

MACCLESFIELD: SO WELL REMEMBERED – Doug Pickford *(£7.95)*

DARK TALES OF OLD CHESHIRE – Angela Conway *(£6.95)*

MAGIC, MYTH AND MEMORIES: The Peak District – Doug Pickford *(£7.95)*

MYTHS AND LEGENDS: East Cheshire and the Moorlands – Doug Pickford *(£7.95)*

SUPERNATURAL STOCKPORT – Martin Mills *(£5.95)*

SHADOWS: a northern investigation of the unknown – Steve Cliffe *(£7.95)*

Sport . . .

RED FEVER:
from Rochdale to Rio as 'United' supporters – Steve Donoghue *(£7.95)*

UNITED WE STOOD:
the unofficial history of the Ferguson years – Richard Kurt *(£6.95)*

MANCHESTER CITY:
Moments to Remember – John Creighton *(£9.95)*

Country Walking . . .

FIFTY CLASSIC WALKS IN THE PENNINES – Terry Marsh *(£8.95)*

RAMBLES IN NORTH WALES – Roger Redfern

HERITAGE WALKS IN THE PEAK DISTRICT – Clive Price

EAST CHESHIRE WALKS – Graham Beech

WEST CHESHIRE WALKS – Jen Darling

WEST PENNINE WALKS – Mike Cresswell